MW01116016

Learn German tor Adult Beginners

Speak German in 30 days!

3 Books in 1

Explore to Win

THIS COLLECTION INCLUDES THE FOLLOWING BOOKS:

Complete German Workbook For Adult Beginners:
Speak German in 30 Days!

German Phrasebook for Adult Beginners:
Over 2500 Essential Words And Phrases You Must Know!

German Short Stories for Adult Beginners: Become Conversational
Today with Fun & Engaging Stories!

$100+ FREE BONUSES

100 German Audio Pronunciations

German Flashcards + 30-Day Study Plan

German Stories Audiobook

German Conversation Dialogues

German Email Crash Course

Premium German Learning Software

Scan QR code to claim your bonuses

— OR —

visit bit.ly/3LrUjlz

© Copyright - All rights reserved.

The content contained within this book may not be reproduced, duplicated, or transmitted without direct written permission from the author or the publisher.

Under no circumstances will any blame or legal responsibility be held against the publisher, or author, for any damages, reparation, or monetary loss due to the information contained within this book, either directly or indirectly.

Legal Notice:

This book is copyright protected. It is only for personal use. You cannot amend, distribute, sell, use, quote, or paraphrase any part, or the content within this book, without the consent of the author or publisher.

Disclaimer Notice:

Please note, the information contained within this document is for educational and entertainment purposes only. All effort has been executed to present accurate, up to date, reliable and complete information. No warranties of any kind are declared or implied. Readers acknowledge that the author is not engaging in the rendering of legal, financial, medical, or professional advice. The content within this book has been derived from various sources. Please consult a licensed professional before attempting any techniques outlined in this book.

By reading this document, the reader agrees that under no circumstances is the author responsible for any losses, direct or indirect, that are incurred as a result of the use of the information contained within this document, including, but not limited to, errors, omissions, or inaccuracies.

BOOK 1

Complete German Workbook
For Adult Beginners

Speak German in 30 days!

Table of Contents

INTRODUCTION

Übung macht den Meister **von** *Helga Daniel*

'Hallo zusammen! Wie geht es Ihnen?'

We are confident that many of you language learners understood the meaning of this statement even without any additional context being provided; after all, it was rather simple, wasn't it? The same is the case with *'von'* in our motivational quote mentioned. *'Von'* is a Dative connector used in German language which means *'from/by/of'*. Look how easy it was, now you all must be wondering what a Dative case is, wait wait! We will get there when the time comes. But for now, what if we told you that learning the German language in 30 days was as simple as this?

We guarantee that after completing and practicing with our **'Speak German in 30 Days bundle'**, you will have no trouble understanding even the most difficult aspects of the German language, be it reading (*Lesen*), writing (*Schreiben*), speaking (*Sprechen*) or listening skills (*Hören*).

Using activities that are concise and simple to grasp, content that is relevant and up to date, sections that provide a quick glimpse of the important information (*Glossar*), activities that are both enjoyable and educational, and many chapters beginning at the A1 level with easy to understand concepts and rules, this course will gradually bring you up to speed in the German language in just 30 days!

We have written this book in the hopes that it would make it simpler for you to learn a new language without the need for a tutor or any additional help. This book is a self-contained guide for all your language needs.

We can assure you that with our **'Speak German in 30 Days bundle',** you will not only be able to perfect your grammar, but you will also be able to understand, read, write, and listen to German content in no time.

Let us give you a sneak peek into the inner workings of our book, which, as we are all aware, is a self-contained guide to learning German in a month. With this book, you will learn the language in 30 days.

To get started, let's talk about some plans that might serve as a foundation for your language learning journey from the very beginning:

- The first chapter *(**Kapitel 1**)* will cover an introduction to the alphabet, basic German phrases, words, as well as their correct pronunciation and phonetics. After that, we will move on to small sentences, greetings, and words, which will provide us with words and vocabulary that are used in day-to-day life and general situations.

- Following the completion of our first chapter, the following one will consist of German counting and numbers with their pronunciation, and short exercises.

- We will begin to present grammatical principles progressively over the course of a period of time.

- There would also be many short stories for you to read as you will gain knowledge of the German language.

- ***Achtung*** columns are designed to provide you with useful tips regarding the German language.

- This book will cover both the concepts taught in the A1 and the A2 levels, which means that after studying with our **'Speak German in 30 Days bundle'**, you will have the ability to deal with day-to-day living in Germany as well as how to introduce yourself and go about your daily life in Germany!

- We will provide you with the best material in the class, including '*Key takeaway*' sections at the end of each chapter to assist you in easily memorizing the most important points.

'ÜBER DEN AUTOR!'

Our author or *'Autor'*, who is responsible for taking out the time and efforts to write this book, has a knack for languages, which suggests that, just like you, the author appreciates the experience of learning about different languages and cultures.

This book is the product of the author's extensive research and analysis of all the various approaches to learning German, followed by careful consideration and selection of the most useful approaches, with the goal of providing you with an educational experience that is on par with the very best that the world has to offer.

We are delighted to begin this adventure with you because we are aware of how important it is to have a trustworthy guiding hand while you are on your trip to learn a new language, and we are looking forward to it. The **'Speak German in 30 Days bundle'** provides you with everything you need to get started on your quest to learn German; you will not require any additional resources to do so.

By the way, are you familiar with the name given to the German language? *'Deutsch'* is the name given to the German language in its official sense. The term *Deutsch* originates from the late Medieval German word **Deudsch**, which derives its meaning from the Early Medieval word **Thiudisk**, which literally translates to **'of the people**.' Hence, it refers to the language that the people actually spoke as opposed to the more formal Latin that was created by the Romans.

Also, fangen wir an! Just look at what we did there! With our **'Speak German in 30 Days Bundle',** you can make learning new languages and switching words into an exciting activity for yourself. This book covers everything you could possibly need to get started on your adventure of learning new languages. We shouldn't waste any more time, so let's jump right into **Kapitel 1** without further ado, shall we?

KAPITEL 1

Ein wahres Fremdwort wird in keiner Sprache heimisch'
von Martin Gerhard Reisenberg

GERMAN ALPHABET AND ITS PRONUNCIATION

Hallo zusammen, Wie geht es Ihnen?

Herzlich willkommen zum Kapitel 1!

You won't have a hard time learning and pronouncing the German alphabets correctly if you're familiar and comfortable with the English alphabet because the two alphabets share a lot of similarities between them.

In addition to all the letters that are found in the English alphabet, the German language also has the characters **ä, ö, ü,** and **ß**.

The majority of the time, the German words are pronounced exactly as they are written, unlike English ones. German sounds that are used in speech conform to a set of rules and patterns. That means, even if you have never heard a German word spoken by a native speaker, you will be able to pronounce it correctly if you learn how to pronounce individual letters and letter combinations correctly as well as where to insert accents.

It is important to keep in mind that the placement of a letter within a German word can cause a change in the way that letter is pronounced within the word. Whenever you need to spell a word, it will help if you are familiar with how to pronounce each letter of the alphabet. In the following table, we will show you how to correctly pronounce each of the German letters and vowels.

ALPHABET	PRONUNCIATION	GERMAN EXAMPLE
A	aah	Address; ah-dress-e (address)
B	bey	Bluse; blooh-ze (blouse)
C	tsey	Sehen; Say-ahn (to see)
D	dey	Damen; Daa-men (women)
E	ey	Ernst; ae-rnst (serious)
F	eff	Frisch; fr-ie-sch (fresh)
G	gey	Gedampft; ge-damm-pft (steamed)
H	ha	Haben; ha-ben (to possess)
I	ee	Immer; ee-mer (always)
J	yot	Jung; yoong (young)
K	kah	Kellner; kelll-ner (waiter)
L	el	Lampe; lamm-pe (lamp)
M	emm	Mann; ma-nn (husband, man)
N	enn	Neben; nay-bun (beside)
O	oh	Ort; oo-rt (place)
P	pey	Paket; pa-ket (packet)
Q	kooh	Quatsch; koo-aa-tsch (nonsense)
R	err	Roman; row-maan (novel)
S	ess	Spielen; shpee-len (to play)
T	tey	Teuer; toy-er (expensive)
U	ooh	Unterlagen; oon-ter-laa-

		gen (documents)
V	fou	Vater; faa-ter (father)
W	weh	Wand; va-and (wall)
X	iks	Fax; fay-x (fax)
Y	ypsilon	System; zers-teym (system)
Z	tset	Zimmer; tsi-mer (room)

Here is how you can correctly pronounce the German letters. The pronunciation of Umlauts are also similar, but first, what are Umlauts? Have you ever seen the letters with two dots on top of them and wondered how to spell them correctly? They are called **'Umlauts'**.

Umlauts are a part of the German alphabet and are used widely in the German **'Sprache'** (*'sh-praa-kh-ey'*). **Umlaut** is the term for the **'ä'** accentuated symbol on the letter 'a' (rhymes with 'zoom out').

Even though **ä**, **ö**, and **ü** can be found at the beginning of some words, you won't typically see them capitalized in the German language. We will learn the **Aussprache** of umlauts later in the chapter along with the sound of tricky vowels.

ACHTUNG!!

Try to stand in front of a mirror and practice the pronunciation of the German alphabets, you can also see how your tongue is shaped while pronouncing each of the letters.

Aktivität (*'ack-tv-tate'*) : After you are done pronouncing the letters, try to sing them aloud and create an alphabet song.

VOWELS

For clarity, the German vowels must be pronounced as precisely and clearly as the consonants. German vowels can sound either long or short. Short sounds are clipped, meaning they are uttered more quickly than in the English language. There are two types of vowels, i.e. long and short, let us quickly go over them.

Long vowels: Vowels that are long are those that are followed by a silent H or are doubled (*Machen, Lohnen, Boot, Seele, Pfuhl*). If a vowel's syllable is not closed by a consonant (*ja, so, ha-ben, o-ben*), or if just one consonant is followed by it, then the vowel is often lengthy (*mut, kam, Not, fön*). Most often, a long I is used to pronounce the combination IE (*Fieber, Schief, Viel*). Except for E, unstressed vowels at the end of words are typically pronounced long (*Schere, Sofa, Vati*).

Short vowels: A emphasized vowel that is accompanied by two consonants is often pronounced short (*Klett, Lacken, Mann, Selber)*, while long vowels that are in their root form retain their length even when they are inflected to be followed by two consonants (*groß-größte or leben-gelebt*). Always a short vowel (*Mock, Trocken, Krücke, Brocken*) comes before '*ck*'. There are a few exceptions to this rule, most of which include unstressed syllables or rather short grammatical terms (e.g. *in, das, von*).

VOWEL	PRONUNCIATION	EXAMPLE
A (short)	Like 'u' in 'cut' only more open and tense.	alle, kann, Land
A (long)	Like 'a' in 'father'	Abend, Jahr, haben
E (short)	Like 'e' in 'met' or in 'pen'	echt, Elch, fertig
E (long)	Like 'a' in 'maid'	Lehrer, leer, legen
I (short)	Like 'i' in 'smitten'	Bild, Gipfel, ich
I (long)	Like 'ee' in 'need'	ihnen, Titel, wider
O (short)	Like 'o' in 'pot'	bockig, toll, Tochter
O (long)	Like 'o' in 'so'	Boden, Ober, rot
U (short)	Like 'oo' in 'foot'	Luft, lustig, unter
U (long)	Like 'oo' in 'wool'	Buch, Kur, ruhig
Ä (short)	closer to a short 'a' in 'land'	Bänder, hätte, Lärm
Ä (long)	Like the 'a' in 'hair'	Mädchen, Käse, täglich
Ö (short)	Like short 'e' with rounded lips, just a little less tense	Hölle, können, Löffel

Ö (long)	Like 'o' in 'short'	Böse, Kröte, Löwe
Ü (short)	Like 'oo' in 'oomph', just a little less stressed	Münze, dünn, drücken
Ü (long)	Like 'oo' in 'oops', bit more stressed	fühlen, Tür, Lüge

There are many books that classify **ä**, **ö**, and **ü** as full-fledged letters, but they are not. For instance, they are not included in the alphabet song that is taught to children in schools in Germany, and they do not have their own sections in dictionaries.

The majority of words that begin with an are derived from 'root' forms that also begin with an a, hence these umlauted forms are closely connected to their non-umlauted counterparts.

ACHTUNG!!

Remember, the German 'i' sounds like the English 'e'. Usually, the German 'e' is soft, like the 'e' in effort or the 'a' in ago.

We hope that by now you must have understood how to pronounce the letters nicely and correctly. Just a bit more and you will learn to speak and pronounce German words in no time!

DIPHTHONGS

Now what exactly are diphthongs? If you merge two vowels into one syllable, you have a diphthong. Consistently, they consist of a single syllable made up of vowels that each have a unique sound. Let's read about some diphthongs in German and learn more about them!

DIPHTHONG	PRONUNCIATION	ENGLISH EXAMPLE	GERMAN EXAMPLE
ai	ay	sky	Mais; m-ay-s (corn)
ei	ay	klein	allein; ae-l-ay-n (alone)
ay	ay	shy	Bayern; b-ay-ern

			(Bavaria)
au	ou	foul	sauer; z-ou-er (sour)
eu	oy	oyster	Leute; l-oy-te (people)
äu	oy	moisture	Häuser; h-oy-zer (houses)
ie	iee	eye	Wiese; v-eei-z-e (meadow)

Now our special case 'ß'

Oh Gott what is that?

The letter **ß**, often known as the 'sharp S,' 'eszett,' or 'Scharfes S,' is the sole letter in the German language that isn't found in the Latin or Roman alphabet. This letter is spoken like the 's' in 'see'.

As to the question of when and where to use ß and ss, it is important to use ss after short vowels [*der Kuss; 'kuuh-ss' (kiss)*] and ß after long vowels [*Tschüß; 'Chew-tsch-ss' (bye)*] and diphthongs.

This may sound illogical, but in most of the cases, you would be trying to pronounce or spell a word that you've already seen or heard, in which case you'll already be aware of whether the vowel is long or short.

PERSONAL PRONOUNS

Personal pronouns are used extensively in both English and German and we are sure many of you are already aware of what personal pronouns are. For example, 'She' is a personal pronoun used in place of a proper name or even a whole (often very long) noun phrase.

'It's Charlotte' could be written as **'she'**

'The young lady in the blue frock' could also be written as **'she'**

'My crush with the dark brown eyes' could also be written as **'she'**

Right? But what about the German personal pronouns and their ***Aussprache***?

Well, the German personal pronouns are a bit more vast than the English language but we will get into those details later, for now, let's just focus on the pronunciation of some German personal pronouns!

- **Ich**; *ee-sch* (remember to make the sound of 'sch' from the back of your throat and make sure that the air also comes out while pronouncing)
- **Du**; *doo-* You (informal)
- **Sie**; *Zee-* She (formal)
- **sie**; *Zee -* (she) (informal)
- **Ihr**; *eeh-ear -* (her)
- **Wir**; *v-ear -* (we) [*keep the 'e' in ear short and quick*]
- **Er**; *air -* (he)
- **Es**; *S -* It (often refers to an object)
- **Mich**; *me-sch* (me)
- **Mir**; *me-ear* (me) [*keep the 'e' in ear short and quick*]
- **Dich**; *D-sch* (you)
- **Dir**; *deer* (you)
- **Euer**; *Oy-er* (your)
- **Ihm**; *Ee-hmm* (him)
- **Ihn**; *Ee-hnn* (him)
- **Uns**; *Oons* (us)
- **Unser**; *OOn-zer* (our)
- **Euch**; *Oy-shh* (you)
- **Ihrer**; *Eeh-rer* (theirs/hers)

These are a few of the most frequently used pronouns of a person in German. Many English terms have multiple German equivalents, as you can see. Therefore, naturally, you're wondering where and how you can put them to use. We'll save the details of the German language's pronouns and case structures for the upcoming chapters.

GERMAN CASES AND ARTICLES

It is very challenging to tell the gender of a noun in German just by looking at the word or its ending. That being the case, learning the gender of German nouns via vocabulary list is the most efficient and convenient method. If you are unsure of the gender of a noun, you can learn the articles or also use a set of rules to find out.

Now, let's just quickly go over the pronunciation of the four German articles **'Der'**, **'Die'**, **'Das'**, and **'Die'**.

- *Der*- 'they-er' this article means masculine words.
- *Die*- 'thee' this article is used for feminine words.
- *Das*- 'tha-ss' this article is used for neutral words.
- *Die*- 'thee' this article is used for plural words.

In your 30 days journey of German language learning you will come across articles with every word. Let's read and try to pronounce some words along with their articles for practice!

- *Das* Auto
- *Der* Große
- *Die* Katze
- *Die* Maus
- *Die* Kleidung
- *Der* Film
- *Die* Sonne
- *Der* Account
- *Das* Backup
- *Die* Erfahrung

Well done! Now for practice, look up all these words and find their meanings along with their correct pronunciation.

ACHTUNG!!

The easiest way to remember the articles is by memorizing them along with the word. You can also make a list of words with articles and memorize them while learning German!

Now for final touches, let's practice pronunciation of day-to-day words and phrases in the German language. Afterwards, we will take a look at some easy greetings and short sentences, and then put our newfound ability of pronunciation to the test, shall we?

So that you may get a feel for the language, let's have a look at some of the most often used terms and verbs together with their *'Aussprache (Owss-spraa-khe).'*

Some of the most common verbs in the German language are:

- **Können**; *'kyo-nun'*- can,
- **Dürfen**; *'dew-r-fun'*- may,
- **Mögen**; *'myo-gun'*- like,
- **Müssen**; *'myu-sun'*- must,
- **Sollen**; *'sow-llen'* - should,
- **Wollen**; *'vo-llen'*- want
- **Antworten**; *'ant-wor-ten'*- to answer
- **Arbeiten**; *'aar-bye-ten'*- to work
- **Bedeuten**; *'bee-doy-ten'*- to mean sth
- **Beginnen**; *'bee-gey-nun'*- to begin
- **Bekommen**; *'bee-common'*- to get sth
- **Bringen**; *'bring-en'*- to bring sth
- **Bleiben**- *'bly-bun'*- to stay
- **Brauchen**- *'brow-ch-unn'*- to need sth
- **Essen**; *'ess-unn'*- to eat
- **Geben**; *'gey-bun'*- to give
- **Gehen**; *'gey-hun'*- to go somewhere
- **Helfen**; *'hell-fun'*- to help with sth
- **Müssen**; *'myu-sun'*- to have to

- *Reisen*; '*rye-sun*'- to travel
- *Lesen*; '*lays-un*'- to read
- *Sagen*; '*zsa-gun*'- to say sth
- *Schaffen*; '*shaa-fun*'- to achieve sth
- *Schreiben*; '*sh-rye-bun*'- to write
- *Setzen*; '*tse-ts-zen*'- to sit
- *Suchen*; '*soo-khun*'- to look for sth
- *Treffen*; '*treś-fun*'- to meet/encounter
- *Trinken*; '*tr-ink-ken*'- to drink
- *Warten*; '*wa-art-ten*'- to wait
- *Wohnen*; '*woh-nun*'- to live

Well, that was easy! Right? With us, you will love the German language. Now just some simple day to day phrases!

- **Ein..Zwei...Drei...Los geht! / 1..2..3..Let's go!**
- Ai-n, ts-wei, dry...low-ss gey-ht
- **Hallo / Hello**
- Haa-low
- **Wie geht's? / How are you?**
- Wee geyh-tss?
- **Guten Morgen / Good Morning**
- Goo-ten More-gun
- **Gute Nacht / Good night**
- Goo-te Nah-kht
- **Guten Abend / Good evening**
- Goo-ten Ah-bend
- **Willkommen / welcome**
- Will-come-enn
- **Tschüß / Bye**
- Chew-tsch-ss
- **Guten Tag / Good day**

- Goo-ten ta-ag
- **Toll / terrific**
- Tow-ll
- **Prima/ Swell**
- Pre-maa

Hush, we are all set now!

Who would have thought learning German could be so enjoyable? Now, as a final step but certainly not the least important one, let's read some simple **loan words** that the German language has adopted from other languages.

LOAN WORDS IN GERMAN LANGUAGE

There are an increasing number of foreign terms used in German, and unfortunately, they frequently violate the pronunciation norms outlined in the two sections that came before this one. They are also called **'borrowed'** words, which means that they are borrowed from another language in German. Many of them are derived from either English or French; nevertheless, even if you are fluent in either language's pronunciation, you will understand most of these words easily!

*Young children attend a **Kindergarten** ('children's garden'). **Gesundheit** does not literally mean 'bless you,' but rather it refers to someone being 'healthy', with the positive sense of the word being conveyed. Psychiatrists talk about **Angst** (fear) and **Gestalt** (shape) psychology, and the word '**kaputt**' is used to describe something that is damaged or broken.*

Words with letters (with the endings 'y' or 'oi') that would not have a distinct pronunciation in German are typically the ones that maintain their original foreign pronunciation. Examples of such words include '**das Baby**' and '**das Croissant.**' There are, without a doubt, a few significant exceptions, but in general this is a clear principle that we should follow.

There are also some words that fall somewhere in the middle. For instance, the word 'cream' (**die Creme**) is pronounced with a long German e in the middle rather than the short è in French; however, many speakers leave the second e silent like they would in French, rather than pronouncing it in German.

Some examples of common loan words in German language:

- das Baby
- der Boss
- das Business
- das Catering
- die City
- der Computer
- das Design
- das Event
- das Fast Food
- das Feeling
- das File
- der Headhunter
- das Hotel
- das Internet
- das Interview
- das Jetlag
- der Job
- der Manager
- das Marketing
- das Meeting
- online
- die Party
- das Shopping
- die Shorts
- die Show
- das Steak
- die Talkshow
- das Team
- der Thriller
- der Tourist
- der Trainer

- das T-Shirt
- der Workshop

Sehr gut!, take that as a compliment! You have now successfully finished studying the German alphabet, vowels, and diphthongs, as well as anything else that you would need to know in order to speak German.

IT'S TIME FOR FUN!

Now that you've mastered the German alphabet and the most basic vocabulary, it's time to put your knowledge to the test with a few quick and easy challenges.

1. **Find the meanings and the articles of the words given below and learn how to pronounce them:**

- _____Auto
- _____Apfel
- _____Volk
- _____Katze
- _____Haar
- _____Hack
- _____Paar
- _____Leben
- _____Umwelt
- _____Umbau
- _____Ecke
- _____Gift
- _____Saal
- _____Buch
- _____Kochbuch

2. **The given text has words from both English and German languages; read it and underline the German words and write their meanings:**

'The Sonne is so bright today, what a Wetter, oh the white Wolken in the Himmel and the rays of the beaming sun, everything is happy about this Ort. The countryside is voller birds and the kids are playing draußen. Oh, how toll. I hoffe that the weather bleibt the same. What a Zeit to be alive!'

Hausaufgabe *(hau-ss-aa-uff-gaa-beh)*: go through all the German words that were discussed in the chapter and attempt to perfect your pronunciation of them.

After the first task of pronunciation, make a list of all the German words that are brought up in the chapter and write their meanings; now that shouldn't be too much homework!

You have done an excellent job at covering the basic vocabulary and their pronunciation in the German language. Now we are left with the German numbers and counting, let us bring that up in **Kapitel 2**!

Bis bald! Alles Gute!

KEY TAKEAWAYS!

*Now we will go over the important concepts that were covered in the **Kapitel 1**!*

In this chapter, we discussed:
- *The German alphabet was one topic that was covered in this chapter.*
- *The vowels that are used in German and the contexts in which they are used.*
- *The most basic ways to pronounce the letters of the German alphabet.*
- *In addition to that, we went over the various personal pronouns.*
- *The use of personal pronouns and the tables that accompany them.*
- *A brief overview of the cases and articles used in the German language.*
- *The most important verbs that are used in daily life, together with their definitions and pronunciations.*

- *A list of common German greetings, complete with their translations and auditory pronunciations.*
- *The concept of borrowing words and the meaning of such words.*
- *Loanwords and borrowed words from other languages that have been adopted into the German language.*

KAPITEL 2

*'Manche Menschen glauben irrtümlich, Intelligent   wäre, die Dummheit ihrer Mitmenschen auszunutzen' **von** Wolfgang J. Reus*

GERMAN NUMBERS AND COUNTING

Hallo zusammen, Wie geht es Ihnen?

Herzlich willkommen zum Kapitel 2!

Hello again, *Wie geht es Ihnen?* I hope you have revised the first chapter nicely, it was pretty fun, right? Now let's move forward to the German numbers. What are numbers or ***Nummers***? Are German numbers different from English numbers, if so, *(Wie)* in what way? Let's find out quickly and easily with the help of our **'Speak German in 30 Days bundle'**.

1..2..3...los geht's!!

We use numbers for little things and also in big scenarios. Want to know the time, want to know the day of the month? Want to understand the amount in your pay cheque? Our day to day life is full of numbers, when we ask someone the time or as we say '***Wie spät ist es?***', their reply comes in numbers, when we buy groceries, we pay the gross amount in numbers, numbers are important and crucial, right?

Knowing how to name numbers and count in the language you're learning is among the most basic things you should be able to do. You can't function in any language without knowing numbers, and you can't live without them. In addition to counting, numbers are used to indicate the date, time, and many other things in our lives.

Let's begin with the basics. A table of the German numbers from 0 to 100 is given below. Take some time to read it, understand the numbers and also how they are pronounced. After that, we will give you some pointers to make sure you remember everything:

NUMBERS FROM 0-20

NUMBER	GERMAN	PRONUNCIATION
0	Null	nool
1	Ein	eyen
2	Zwei	ts-why
3	Drei	dry
4	Vier	fear
5	Fünf	fyunf
6	Sechs	zecks
7	Sieben	zee-bun
8	Acht	aa-kht
9	Neun	noyn
10	Zehn	tsyen
11	Elf	elf
12	Zwölf	ts-wolf
13	Dreizehn	dry-tsyen
14	Vierzehn	fear-tsyen
15	Fünfzehn	fyunf-tsyen
16	Sechzehn	zeiss-tsyen
17	Siebzehn	zeeb-tsyen
18	Achtzehn	aa-kht-tsyen
19	Neunzehn	noun-tsyen

20	Zwanzig	tswan-zig

Although I'll give a quick tip for memorizing these numbers later in the chapter, there are no rules for these numbers. And it's important to have these numbers in memory since they appear in every number you'll use for counting, in one way or another.

For example, just as *'nine'* is present in *'nineteen'*, *'ninetyeight'*, 'ninety' and *'nine hundred'*, the same can be said for *'neun'* (**'nine'**) in German. *'Neunzehn'*, *'neunundzwanzig'*, *'neunzig'* and *'neunhundert'*.

ACHTUNG!!

To form sechzehn, -s is dropped from 'sechs' and -en is dropped from the 'sieben' to form siebzehn. These are some of the little things which you will get used to when you learn the language.

NUMBERS FROM 21-50

NUMBERS	GERMAN	PRONUNCIATION
21	Einundzwanzig	eyen-oond-tswan-zig
22	Zweiundzwanzig	tsvy-oond-tswan-zig
23	Dreiundzwanzig	dry-oond-tswan-zig
24	Vierundzwanzig	fear-oond-tswan-zig
25	Fünfundzwanzig	fyun-f-oond-tswan-zig
26	Sechsundzwanzig	zecks-oond-tswan-zig
27	Siebenundzwanzig	sea-bun-oond-tswan-zig
28	Achtundzwanzig	aa-kht-oond-tswan-zig
29	Neunundzwanzig	nyon-oond-tswan-zig
30	Dreißig	dry-tsig
31	Einunddreißig	eyen-oond-dry-tsig

32	Zweiunddreißig	tsvy-oond-dry-tsig
33	Dreiunddreißig	dry-oond-dry-tsig
34	Vierunddreißig	fear-oond-dry-tsig
35	Fünfunddreißig	fyunf-oond-dry-tsig
36	Sechsunddreißig	zecks-oond-dry-tsig
37	Siebenunddreißig	sea-bun-oond-dry-tsig
38	Achtunddreißig	aa-kht-oond-dry-tsig
39	Neununddreißig	nyon-oond-dry-tsig
40	Vierzig	fear-tsig
41	Einundvierzig	eyen-oond-fear-tsig
42	Zweiundvierzig	tsvy-oond-fear-tsig
43	Dreiundvierzig	dry-oond-fear-tsig
44	Vierundvierzig	fear-oond-fear-tsig
45	Fünfundvierzig	fyunf-oond-fear-tsig
46	Sechsundvierzig	zecks-oond-fear-tsig
47	Siebenundvierzig	sea-bun-oond-fear-tsig
48	Achtundvierzig	aa-kht-oond-fear-tsig
49	Neunundvierzig	nyon-oond-fear-tsig
50	Fünfzig	fyunf-oond-fear-tsig

ACHTUNG!!

Between forty and ninety, all the numbers are regular. They take the first four letters of the number between one and ten and add the word 'zig' to the end of it.

You're probably used to saying '*twenty-one*' if you speak English. Yet, they reverse the order and say '*one and twenty*' in German. Also, the German language combines everything into a single word. Fortunately, it's easy to get the hang of once you start learning! Look at these few examples to make it even simpler:

ein + und + zwanzig one + and + twenty	21
zwei + und + zwanzig two + and + twenty	22
drei + und + dreißig three + and + thirty	33
vier + und + achtzig four + and + eighty	84

Even easier numbers: The hundreds

The '*hundreds*' in both German and English are very similar in nature, we are sure that you will also remember them easily, let's have a look:

NUMBERS	GERMAN	PRONUNCIATION
100	hundert	hoond-ert
200	zweihundert	tsvy-hoond-ert
300	dreihundert	dry-hoond-ert
400	vierhundert	fear-hoond-ert
500	fünfhundert	fyunf-hoond-ert

600	sechshundert	zecks-hoond-ert
700	siebenhundert	zee-bun-hoond-ert
800	achthundert	aa-kht-hoond-ert
900	neunhundert	nyon-hoond-ert

ACHTUNG!!

The hundred number is always spoken first. You pronounce it the same way you would in English between 100 and 119. This makes 102 ('one hundred and two') into 'einhundertundzwei'.

The number-swapping rule kicks in once you reach a number higher than 20, but only for two-digit numerals. The number 128 ('one hundred and twenty-eight') is therefore converted to 'einhundertachtundzwanzig'.

And the thousands (*tausende*) also follow the same pattern:

1000	tausend	taow-send
2000	zweitausend	tsvy-taow-send
3000	dreitausend	dry-taow-send
4000	viertausend	fear-taow-send
5000	fünftausend	fyunf-taow-send
10000	zehntausand	tsyen-taow-send
20000	zwanzigtausend	tswan-zig-taow-send
One million	eine Million	Eyene mili-own

'One': Ein, Eins, Eine, Einen, Eines, Einer oder Einem?

The only number that has to be changed in German is **one** or **1.**

We have three terms in English for 'one'. The word *'one'* itself or the letters *'a'* or *'an'* can be used to indicate that there is just one of something.

'I have one brother.'
'I have a sister.'
'I have an apple.'

Variations of *'ein'* and *'eins'* are used to express these three nouns in German.

The *'eins'* version of the word, which is the number one itself, is always used when counting the quantity of something, such as the number of persons in a group, as you can see in the table at the beginning of this article.

But, you should use the *'ein'* form of the word and its case-based derivatives when you're talking about anything else. Do not be alarmed, we will take the German cases in detail in the coming chapters, for now just remember the endings in different cases, Such as:

Nominative case:
Masculine: **ein** *Bruder ('a Brother')*
Neutral: **ein** *Auto ('a Car')*
Feminine: **eine** *Schwester ('a Sister')*

Accusative case:
Masculine: **einen** *Bruder*
Neutral: **ein** *Auto*
Feminine: **eine** *Schwester*

Dative case:
Masculine: **einem** *Bruder*
Neutral: **einem** *Auto*
Feminine: **einer** *Schwester*

Genitive case:

Masculine: *eines* *Bruders*

Neutral: *eines* *Autos*

Feminine: *einer* *Schwester*

ACHTUNG!!

Some numbers, such as the German equivalents of 'zwei' (two) and 'drei' (three), don't require any changes and remain the same throughout.

We have now covered all the basics of counting and numbers in our **'Speak German in 30 Days bundle'**, and we hope that you enjoyed learning them as well. It wasn't so difficult, was it? Let's engage in some fun activities and exercises to work on pronouncing the numbers and help you to remember them as well.

1..2..3..los geht's!!

Aktivitäten:

1. **Read these German kids rhymes with numbers and practice your pronunciation, after you are done, write the translation of the given rhymes in english:**

   Eins, zwei, Polizei
   drei, vier, Offizier
   fünf, sechs, alte Hex'
   sieben, acht, gute Nacht!
   neun, zehn, auf Wiedersehen!

   _____

   _____

_____

_____

_____

_____

Eins, zwei, Papagei

drei, vier, Grenadier

fünf, sechs, alte Hex'

sieben, acht, Kaffee gemacht

neun, zehn, weiter geh'n

elf, zwölf, junge Wölf'

dreizehn, vierzehn, Haselnuss

fünfzehn, sechzehn, du bist duss.

_____

_____

_____

_____

_____

_____

_____

_____

2. **Write the english meanings of the mentioned words and also write down the numbers mentioned:**

- *Vier Papageie* _____
- *Zwei Grenadiere* _____
- *Sieben Kaffee* _____
- *Fünf Jungs* _____
- *Zwölf Haselnüsse* _____
- *Drei Offiziere* _____
- *Dreizehn Pulli* _____
- *Zwanzig Orangen* _____
- *Neun Bananen* _____
- *Hundert Pakete* _____

1. Now answer these easy questions to make your knowledge of the German numbers even more **stark**:

- *Was ist zwei plus fünf? (2 + 5)*

  _____

- *Was ist elf minus sieben? (11 – 7)*

  _____

- *Was ist fünf minus vier? (5 – 4)*

  _____

- *Wie alt bist du?*

  _____

- *Wie viele Bananen sind in einem Dutzend? (Dozen)*

  _____

3. Write down the German counting from:
- 100-150
- 550-750

- 95-200
- 320-500
- 1290-1350

4. Write down the German counting for the given numbers below:

- 84 _____
- 46 _____
- 36 _____
- 23 _____
- 49 _____
- 32 _____
- 63 _____
- 72 _____
- 86 _____
- 92 _____
- 10 _____
- 80 _____
- 21 _____
- 27 _____
- 74 _____
- 72 _____
- 55 _____
- 88 _____
- 22 _____
- 99 _____
- 11 _____
- 33 _____
- 22 _____
- 73 _____
- 98 _____
- 46 _____

- 100 _____
- 350 _____
- 250 _____
- 150 _____
- 200 _____
- 400 _____
- 700 _____
- 500 _____
- 130 _____
- 384 _____
- 715 _____
- 846 _____
- 294 _____
- 902 _____
- 2000 _____
- 3826 _____
- 9582 _____
- 6740 _____
- 4000 _____
- 2746 _____
- 5390 _____
- 3000 _____
- 7286 _____
- 9163 _____
- 4299 _____
- 3649 _____
- 9000 _____
- 1735 _____
- 8478 _____
- 3862 _____
- 2023 _____
- 1184 _____

- 2011 _____

- 4756 _____

- 4863 _____

Sehr gut! You have completed the task of learning about the German numbers, and you should feel proud of yourself. We sure hope that you were able to learn about numbers in a way that was both enjoyable and not too challenging. Well, as promised, with our '**Learn German in 30 days Bundle**' you will be a master of the language soon!

We all know how to tell time in English, right? It's not too difficult and almost everyone knows how to tell the time in English. But what about the German language? How do we tell the time in German? Let's find out about the time now and learn how to say it in German. **Los geht's!**

Telling the time in German!

Wieviel Uhr ist es? (*we-feel oohr ist ess?*) oder **Wie spät ist es?** (*we sh-paet ist ess?*)

You will hear these sentences a lot in Germany. Germans are regarded for being very punctual, we know that right? It is usually considered rude when you show up late at an event in Germany. What if you find yourself in such a condition and ask some native German guy for help? How would you do it, what would you say? Well, you can start by asking '**Wie spät ist es?**', which roughly translates to '*How late is it?*' It is the most typical approach to inquire about the time in German. Typically, neither '*What time is it?*' nor '*How early is it?*' are polite questions to ask.

ACHTUNG!!

The German term for time is 'Zeit' [tsey-it], which has entered English as a component of the noun 'Zeitgeist', which is frequently used to describe the main mood of a certain time period. Thus, many English speakers are familiar with it. It's interesting to note, though, that there is no way to inquire for the time in German that really uses the word 'Zeit'. Always remember this when you ask a German about time.

To tell the time in German you have to follow some simple and basic rules, let's know more about them first. Start with '**Es ist**' (*It is*) and follow these basic rules:

- *If it's at the top of the hour, give the number of the appropriate hour + the word* **Uhr** *(o'clock).*
  Zum Beispiel:
  '**Es ist ein Uhr**' (It is 1 o'clock).
  '**Es ist neun Uhr**' (It is 9 o'clock).

- *To express minutes before the hour, give the number of minutes +* **vor** *(to, before) + the hour.*
  Zum Beispiel:
  '**Es ist zwanzig vor neun**' (It is 8:40)
  '**Es ist fünf vor zwölf**' (It is 11:55)

- *To express minutes after the hour, give the number of minutes +* **nach** *(past, after) + the hour.*
  Zum Beispiel:
  '**Es ist zehn nach drei**' (It is 3:10)
  '**Es ist siebzehn nach fünf**' (it is 5:17)

- *To express halfway to the hour, use the word* **halb** *(half). Zum Beispiel:*
  '**Es ist halb acht**' (It is 7:30)
  '**Es ist fünf vor halb sieben**' (It is 6:25)
  '**Es ist zehn nach halb zehn**' (It is 10:40)

- *To tell time using quarter, use the word* **Viertel** *(quarter) followed by* **vor** *or* **nach** *and then the appropriate hour. Zum Beispiel:*
  '**Es ist Viertel nach zwei**' (It is 2:15)
  '**Es ist Viertel vor neun**' (It is 8:45)

- *To express noon and midnight, use the following expressions. Zum Beispiel:*
  '**Es ist Mittag**' (It is noon)
  '**Es ist Mitternacht**' (It is midnight)

Aktivitäten:

Try to solve these quick exercises and sharpen your knowledge!

1. **write down the given time in expressions:**

- 1:00 Uhr _____
- 4:00 Uhr _____
- 2:16 Uhr _____
- 8:00 Uhr _____
- 8:28 Uhr _____
- 9:30 Uhr _____
- 2:45 Uhr _____
- 4:20 Uhr _____
- 8:45 Uhr _____
- 6:00 Uhr _____
- 4:45 Uhr _____
- 6:30 Uhr _____
- 10:00 Uhr _____
- 12:00 Uhr _____
- 17:00 Uhr _____
- 22:50 Uhr _____
- 16:30 Uhr _____
- 12:50 Uhr _____
- 14:45 Uhr _____
- 19:34 Uhr _____
- 15:00 Uhr _____
- 23:50 Uhr _____
- 11:20 Uhr _____
- 10:30 Uhr _____
- 15:42 Uhr _____

- 18:00 Uhr _____

- 20:00 Uhr _____

2. Now tell the time by looking at these wall clocks!

Um..Entschuldigung, wie spät ist es?

1. _____

2. _____

3. _____

4. _____

5. _____

6. _____

7. _____

8. _____

9. _____

1. _____

2. _____

3. _____

4. _____

5. _____

6. _____

7. _____

8. _____

9. _____

SOME COMMON TIME RELATED EXPRESSIONS

Super!! Now that we have learned all about the time and different ways to express it. We hope it has not been stressful so far, with our **'Speak German in 30 Days bundle'** you will have fun as well as learn in no time!

Now what about the daily slangs related to time? In the table below, you will find some easy time expressions which would be very beneficial in your day to day life:

EXPRESSION	MEANING
an hour	*eine Stunde*
in an hour	*In einer Stunde*
a minute	*eine Minute*
a second	*eine Sekunde*
quarter an hour	*eine viertel Stunde*
Half an hour	*eine halbe Stunde*
At what time	*um wieviel Uhr?*
At exactly midnight	*Genau um Mitternacht*
At exactly 3:00	*Genau um drei Uhr*
At about 3:00	*um ungefähr/etwa drei Uhr*
Until 3:00	*Bis drei Uhr*
After 3:00	*Nach drei Uhr*
Before 3:00	*vor drei Uhr*
In the morning	*am Morgen*

In the afternoon	*am Nachmittag*
In the evening	*am Abend*
Since when?	*Seit wann?*
An hour ago	*Vor einer Stunde*
Every hour	*Jede Stunde*

EXPRESSING DATES

The days of the week are very similar between German and English. Whereas most days of the week in English end in the word *'day'*, most days in German finish in the word **'Tag'** (with Wednesday being the exception; it is Mittwoch). The translation of *'day'* is **'Tag'** *(Taa-aag)*, as you can probably already guess. Now we will dive deeper in the dates, days and months of the German language with their pronunciations:

ENGLISH	GERMAN	PRONUNCIATION
Monday	*Montag*	maun-tag
Tuesday	*Dienstag*	deens-tag
Wednesday	*Mittwoch*	mit-wo-kh
Thursday	*Donnerstag*	donners-tag
Friday	*Freitag*	fry-tag
Saturday	*Samstag*	saams-tag
Sunday	*Sonntag*	sonn-tag
January	*Januar*	janua-r
February	*Februar*	februa-r
March	*März*	mae-rz
April	*April*	april
May	*Mai*	may

June	*Juni*	you-ni
July	*Juli*	you-li
August	*August*	ow-gust
September	*September*	zeptember
October	*Oktober*	ocktober
November	*November*	november
December	*Dezember*	detz-ember
Spring	*der Frühling*	frooh-ling
Summer	*der Sommer*	zommer
Autumn	*der Herbst*	hay-erb-st
Winter	*der Winter*	winter

ACHTUNG!!

The weeks' days and the months' names all begin with the definite article 'der' since they are all masculine nouns. Yet you often don't use them with an article in a sentence. For instance:

'Heute ist Freitag' (Today is Friday)

'Es ist Oktober' (It is October)

'Es ist Sommer' (It is Summer)

'Es ist Herbst' (It is Autumn)

Aktivitäten:

1. **Write down the following words in German with their articles:**

June _____

April _____

May _____

January _____

Summer _____

October _____

Autumn _____

January _____

July _____

September _____

December _____

Friday _____

Sunday _____

Monday _____

Winter _____

2. Write the english translation of the given rhymes and also write the english meanings of the months mentioned in the rhyme:

Es war eine Mutter,
die hatte vier Kinder:
den Frühling, den Sommer,
den Herbst und den Winter.

Der Frühling bringt Blumen,
Der Sommer den Klee,
Der Herbst, der bringt Trauben,
Der Winter den Schnee.

_____

_____

_____

_____

_____

_____

_____

_____

_____

_____

_____

_____

_____

Toll! You have finally reached the point where you are able to tell time in German. Was it fun? ***Ja?*** We knew it! Now that you understand what's happening and how to tell the time in German, what are you going to say if a native German asks you the time? You no longer need to be worried about that, we got you covered!

Before concluding the chapter, we have one puzzle for you.
The letter *'U'* in the word *'Uhr'* is always written with a capital letter. ***Warum? (do you know why)*** What exactly is the reason for that? Let's find out the answer to that quickly; all you need to know are a few basics, and you'll be good to go. ***Fangen wir an!***

As everyone is familiar with, the first letter of the first word in an English sentence must always be capitalized. However, there are some exceptions, such as nouns, which should always begin with a capital letter.
How does the German language function? We are familiar with the ***Alphabet*** and ***Nummers***, which are the building blocks of the German language, but what about punctuation? Are they the same as the English language, then? Let's find out!

CAPITALIZATION & GERMAN PUNCTUATION

German and English capitalization styles are typically close or identical. Of course, every rule has exceptions. Learning these rules is essential for proper grammar if you wish to learn and write German well.

It can be challenging at first to get accustomed to new phrases and grammar, the overwhelming set of rules, the big sentences and so many rules, but that's exactly why we are helping you with our **'Speak German in 30 Days bundle'**. We know that German can appear odder than most languages when written down. More importantly, what's with all the capital letters, though? Don't worry, we are here to your rescue! ***Los Gehts!***

Zuerst, how do we capitalize the German language?

German and English capitalization styles are typically close or identical. Of course, every rule has exceptions. Learning these rules is essential for proper grammar if you wish to write German well. Let's take a closer look.

How do you capitalize words in German?

German capitalize ***alle*** *nouns*! You probably don't need me to tell you that writing in both upper- and lowercase letters (known as case distinction) is a common phenomenon in many languages and that it serves as a signal for a grammar rule, such as starting a new sentence. There are also many other rules which you can easily keep in mind. We have made a quick list for you to learn:

- The formal you, *'Sie'*, is capitalized at all times. However, the reflexive pronoun **sich** is excluded from this, but not the related forms ***Ihnen*** and ***ihr***.
- The first-person singular pronoun *'ich'* is not capitalized unless it starts a sentence, unlike the English ***I***.
- Unlike in English, adjectives describing nationality, ethnicity and religion are not capitalized in German unless they're part of a proper noun ***zum Beispiel*** (for example) ***'Deutsche Bank'***.
- The order of decimal points and commas when writing numbers is the same as the rest of continental Europe (for example, a Kaffee might cost *1,50€* whereas a car might cost *15.000€*).

Now coming back to the topic of nouns. As we already mentioned, all nouns are capitalized. This includes both proper nouns and gerund nouns in case the word *'alle'* is still causing you to have doubts. We will discuss this deeply later in the course! But for now, remember the basics.

Gerund nouns are adjectives or verbs that serve as nouns but are not proper nouns. Importantly, they are still capitalized since they are also counted as nouns. ***Alle nouns!***

Proper nouns:
- *das Kind (the child)*
- *das Auto (the car)*

Gerund nouns:
- *essen (to eat) - das Essen (food/eating)*
- *fahren (to run) - das Rennen (race/running)*

Acktivität:

1. **Do you want to learn a simple and cool trick to practice punctuation? Try to recognize all the nouns in this sentence and write them down with their meanings, (we know that you barely understand the meaning of the sentence but we are sure that you can still identify all the nouns)**

   'Es sind vier Stifte und drei Katzen in meiner Tasche'

Rules of German Capitalisation:

- **Proper Nouns**

  Proper nouns, which are usually capitalized, include words used for people, places, streets, movies, books, etc. Only the first letter of the word is capitalized if the noun is a compound word (made up of many words), such as ***Haustier*** rather than ***HausTier***.

- **Pronoun capitalization**

  Pronouns are typically not capitalized. However, there are two exceptions. In a formal situation, the capitalized pronoun ***'Sie'*** indicates 'you' as opposed to the 'you' in informal situations which can be simply written as ***'sie'***.

- However, it's common to capitalize the pronouns ***'du'*** and ***'ihr'*** when addressing someone in writing, but it's not mandatory. If you don't do that, you won't be seen as unfriendly!

- German never uses the ***'Oxford comma'*** at the end of a list.

- **Verbs or Adjectives as Nouns (Nominalisation)**

  Gerunds are words that serve as nouns but are actually adjectives or verbs rather than proper nouns. They are likewise capitalized in German because they function like nouns.
- For verbs that frequently double as nouns, such as ***das Schwimmen, das Tanzen, das Gehen, oder das Schreiben,*** capitalization can be very useful. The fact that they start with a capital letter makes it simple to recognize them.

Lets understand it better with the help of these easy example:

'Wussten Sie, dass Jan gerade ein neues deutsches Auto gekauft hat? Es ist ein Mercedes. Die erste Fahrt war erstaunlich! Es ist sein ganzer Stolz.'

'Es sind vier Stifte und drei Katzen in meiner Tasche'

The majority of German capitalization laws are used in these examples, which includes proper nouns, nouns, pronouns, verbs used as nouns, and both uncapitalized and capitalized adjectives. Don't worry, we have made it as simple as it could be for you!

ACHTUNG!!

'Das ist wirklich genauso, äh, für jemand [jemanden], der vielleicht nur mal auf eine Tasse Kaffee bei uns in der schönen Lobby sitzen möchte...'

The words 'jemanden' and 'der' are not capitalized in the next sentence. Pronouns don't start with a capital letter like nouns do ('das' is capitalized, of course, because it is the first word in the sentence). Yet, 'die Lobby' and both of the nouns in 'eine Tasse Kaffee' are capitalized.

Let us also look at the workings of punctuation marks in the German language, follow this table:

GERMAN	ENGLISH	MARK
die Anführungszeichen	quotation marks	' ' or « »
die Auslassungspunkte	ellipsis dots	...
das Ausrufezeichen	exclamation mark	!
der Apostroph	apostrophe	'
der Bindestrich	hyphen	-
der Doppelpunkt/ das Kolon	colon	:
der Ergänzungsstrich	dash	-
das Fragezeichen	question mark	?
der Gedankenstrich	long dash	—
runde Klammern	parentheses	()
eckige Klammern	brackets	[ ]
das Komma	comma	,
der Punkt	period	.
das Semikolon	semicolon	;

IT'S TIME FOR FUN!

Now that you've mastered the German numbers and the capitalization and punctuation, it's time to put your knowledge to the test with a few quick and easy challenges. ***Los geht's!***

1. **Find 10 mistakes in this text. Be careful with Uppercase letters and lowercase letters.**

'Lieber Florian!

Gestern war ich in berlin. Ich habe den fernsehturm gesehen. Es hat mir viel spaß gemacht. Aber ich war nicht Allein, sondern mit meinen freunden zusammen; Sie waren auch sehr begeistert. Wir haben vieles unternommen, sind viel Gelaufen. Wir waren alle sehr Müde. Besonders Heiko, der in der U-Bahn eingeschlafen ist. Es war lustig. Wir haben viel gelacht! Mir hat die Berliner mauer gefallen, aber die anderen haben Sie nicht so gemocht wie ich, weil ihnen zu kalt war. Im januar ist berlin ziemlich kalt! Nächstes Mal komme ich im sommer.
Liebe Grüße,
Deine Janina'

2. Identify the words in the given text which need to be capitalized and capitalize them:

Es waren einmal vor langer zeit ein vogel und ein wal. Herr vogel liebte frau wal. Und frau wal liebte herrn vogel. Herr vogel liebte frau wals hübsches lächeln. Er liebte es, wie sie so elegant durchs wasser schwamm. Frau wal liebte herrn vogels prächtige weiße federn. Sie liebte es, ihm zuzuschauen, wie er durch den himmel flog. Sie beide liebten es, viele winzige fische zu fressen.

_____

_____

_____

_____

_____

3. Write down the German meanings with articles of the given words:

- Car   _____
- Table   _____
- Spoon   _____
- Chair   _____
- Summer   _____
- Airplane   _____

- Curtains   _____
- Windows   _____
- Door   _____
- Book   _____
- Walking   _____
- Running   _____
- Eating   _____
- Home   _____
- Environment   _____
- Mobile phone   _____
- Fish   _____
- Laptop   _____
- School   _____
- Fridge   _____
- Washing machine   _____
- Tubelight   _____
- Pen   _____
- Lipstick   _____
- Charger   _____
- Watch   _____
- Dog   _____
- Chocolate   _____
- Gift   _____

Toll! You have successfully completed the first step towards learning German by mastering its most fundamental concepts, including the alphabet, numbers, punctuation, time telling, and *mehr*. *Wir hoffen* that you enjoyed yourself as much as we did, *oder?* What has so far been your favorite part?

But try not to get your hopes up. We still have a long way to go, but with our **'Learn German in 30 days bundle,'** we are confident that not only will you learn German in just 30 days, but that you will also have a great deal of fun doing it!

The *German greetings*, *Articles*, and *Nouns* are also some of the fundamental building blocks of the German language; let's get started with them in **Kapitel 3** by focusing on these!

Bis bald! Alles Gute!

KEY TAKEAWAYS!

*Now we will talk about the important concepts that were covered in **Kapitel 2!***

In this chapter, we went through the following topics:

- *The German numbers.*
- *The names of the numbers in German and how they should be spoken.*
- *A tutorial on the basics of German numbering writing.*
- *We also learned how to tell and ask the time in German.*
- *We also learned how to tell and ask the time in German.*
- *The basics of the German language regarding the time, including how to inquire about it, what to inquire about, and how to correctly pronounce it.*
- *Expressive idioms and phrases commonly associated with the passage of time*
- *A rundown on the various ways dates can be expressed in German.*
- *The practice of capitalizing German words and nouns in their proper context.*
- *The proper way to capitalize words in the German language.*
- *Few introductory remarks concerning the capitalization of proper nouns and pronouns.*
- *The rules for capitalizing verbs, adjectives, and other words depending on whether they are used as nouns.*
- *German punctuation marks and their signs, coupled with the pronunciations of those marks and the meanings of those markings in English.*

ANTWORTEN! ANSWER KEY

1. (page 32)

    One, two, police

    Three, four, officer,

    Five, six, old witch

    Seven, eight, good night!

    Nine, ten, goodbye!

    One, two, parrot

    Three, four, grenadier

    Five, six, old witch

    Seven, eight, coffee made

    Nine, ten, go on

Eleven, twelve, young wolf

Thirteen, fourteen, hazelnut

Fifteen, sixteen, you're a nut.

2. (page 44)

There was a mother,

who had four children:

spring, summer,

autumn and winter.

The spring brings flowers,

Summer brings clover,

Autumn brings grapes,

The winter the snows.

January, February, March, April,

The annual clock never stands still.

May, June, July, August,

awakens in all of us the love of life.

September, October, November, December

And then, and then, the whole thing starts

starts all over again.

2. (page 52)

- Zeit
- Vogel
- Wal
- Vogel
- Frau
- Wal
- Herrn
- Vogel
- Vogel
- Frau
- Wals
- Wasser
- Wal
- Herrn

- Vogels
- Himmel
- Fische

KAPITEL 3

*Schulnoten sind nichts anderes als Kleingeld **von** Manfred Züfle*

GREETINGS!!

Hallo zusammen, Wie geht es Ihnen?

Herzlich willkommen zum Kapitel 3!

What are these two sentences which appear at the starting of every chapter? These are also greetings which we use to welcome you to the new chapter.

It is widely known that greetings occupy a significant place in our daily lives. They can be found just about everywhere! Whether we run into a ***Freund*** or meet ***neue Leute***, we always make sure to greet our ***Eltern***, our friends, and everyone else we come across.

These are not just available in German, but also in each and every ***Sprache*** that is spoken on the planet. The greetings are constructed out of several elements such as ***Wörter***, nouns, expressions, phrases, and other such ***dinge***. We aim to make these easy to learn and memorize for you with the help of our **'Speak German in 30 Days bundle'.**

In the ***letztes Kapitel***, we discussed the basics, such as pronunciation, the alphabet, Capitalization and numbers; now, let's delve into some more advanced topics, such as German greetings, nouns, articles, yes and no, please and thank you, and everything else associated with this topic.

Sind Sie gespannt? Wir sind es auf jeden Fall! Fangen wir jetzt an!
(Are you excited? We sure are! Let's get started!)

In all **Sprachen**, a noun refers to a person, object, place, or concept. Yet, there are some distinctions between German and English nouns. First, every noun in **Deutsch** has a gender. They might be **neuter**, **male**, or **feminine**. Moreover, they are frequently followed by an article, which can be **die, der,** or **das** depending on the gender. And as we all already know, **all German nouns are all capitalized**.

NOUNS, GREETINGS AND ARTICLES

Learning proper German greetings and farewells is a respectful way to start conversations with native German speakers. Understanding the cultural context of German words and phrases is an integral part of learning the language. There are polite and casual ways to say **'Hallo'** and **'Tschüss'** in German.

The ability to welcome and greet people nicely in German will pave the way for more meaningful friendships and acceptance amongst people who speak this language. When it comes to greetings and farewells in German, both formal and informal options exist. We'll analyze a number of options, so you can pick the best one.

Los geht's!

First questions first, What is a noun and how does it affect the 'gender' of the words?

A noun is always either *feminine, masculine,* or *neuter,* whether it be animate or inanimate. The grammatical gender of a noun typically corresponds to its gender in nature. For example, the noun **Herr** - the German word for *'man'* - is masculine and the noun **Frau** - the German word for a *'woman'*.

The issue is that, especially when the noun is inanimate or a concept, what the word refers to doesn't always help in determining its grammatical gender. There are a few techniques you can use to assist you determine a noun's gender, even if there are no clear guidelines or explanations for doing so.
But with the help of our **'Speak German in 30 Days bundle'**, we will make it easy for you to ace this **Thema** also.

But first, let's have a look at some basic **Begrüßungen** in German and English, Have a look at the given table:

GERMAN	ENGLISH	PRONUNCIATION
Hallo!	*Hello*	haa-low
Guten Morgen!	*Good morning!*	Goot-en morgue-en
Guten Tag!	*Good day!*	Goot-en taa-ag
Grüß Gott!	*Good day!* (Used mostly in southern Germany and Austria)	Groos- gott
Guten Abend!	*Good evening!*	Goot-en Aa-bund
Auf Wiedersehen!	*See you next time!*	Owf- weeder- seyehn
Tschüss!	*Bye !*	tsch-uu-ss
Ciao!	*Bye !*	chaa-ow
Ja	*Yes*	ya
Nein	*No*	nine
Vielleicht	*Maybe*	feel-eyei-scht
danke	*thank you*	daan-kae
bitte	*please*	bit-tay
Entschuldigung	*I'm sorry, excuse me*	Ent- school- digung
Wie gehts?	*How are you?*	We gey-hts?
und	*and*	oond
oder	*or*	ode-er
aber	*but*	aa-bur
weil	*because*	why-isle
hier	*here*	hear
da	*there*	daa

Aktivität:

1. **Answer these simple questions and practice your knowledge of German greetings!**

- How would you say goodbye in German to the carwash employee when you leave after getting your car washed?
    - Guten Morgen!
    - Hallo!
    - Mahlzeit
    - Tschüss

- Imagine that you're inside a German bank in Munich to withdraw money from an ATM. One of the security guards in the bank greets you with a warm smile that makes your day as you walk into the bank. What sort of greeting might you hear him or her say?
    - Gute Nacht
    - Auf Wiederhören
    - Guten Tag
    - Servus

- Imagine that you are at a restaurant in Hamburg for a nice lunch. As you walk towards a table, how might you greet people who are passing by?
    - Guten Nachmittag
    - Mahlzeit
    - Hallo
    - bis bald!

- Which of the following questions would you use only among close friends and relatives?
    - Wie heißen Sie?
    - Wie geht es Ihnen?
    - Wie finden Sie...
    - Wie geht's?

2. Arrange the following in correct order

- GTUNE AGT   _____
- GTUEN ANEBD   _____
- GTUE ANCTH   _____
- HLOLA   _____
- IEW HTGE'S   _____
- ILELVCTHEI   _____
- RODE   _____
- BAER   _____
- NSHLIGNGETCUDU   _____

ACHTUNG!!

The Germans are all about efficiency, they try to waste as little time as possible so they often shorten their greetings to a single word. Try some of the shortened greetings:

- Morgen!

- Tag!

- Abend!

ARTICLES IN GERMAN LANGUAGE

An **Artikel** (*article*) is a word that goes with a noun and indicates whether it is (**das**) *neuter*, (**der**) *masculine*, or (**die**) *feminine*. The best approach to discern the gender of a German noun is to learn the noun with the article. There are three simple articles in the German language which you should always remember, they are '*der, die and das*'. There is also a plural article 'die', we will discuss these in depth in this **Kapitel!**

Let's start with the most basic question, How do you use the German articles **(der, die, das)?**

Making sure you understand the basic concepts underlying the words '*der, die, and das*' is the first and most important step in learning the various articles. Every noun in German is given one of three genders: *masculine (männlich), feminine (weiblich), or neuter (sächlich).*

It is essential to understand which form of '*the*' is used for each gender before continuing. In German, the word '*der*' is used for masculine nouns, '*die*' is used for feminine nouns, and '*das*' is used for neuter nouns.

It's also crucial to realize that the gender of a noun is assigned to the word, not the person, thing, or object, which makes it challenging to predict the gender of a given noun from a noun's context.

Zum Beispiel, the word for '*table*' in German is masculine (*der Tisch*), whereas the term for '*car*' is neuter (*das Auto*). *Glücklicherweise*, you can find some patterns to guide you.

The following table lists the *bestimmt* and *unbestimmt* articles in the German language, much like in English.

	FEMININE	MASCULINE	NEUTER	PLURAL
DEFINITE ARTICLE (*the*)	Die	Der	Das	Die
INDEFINITE ARTICLE (*a, an*)	Eine	Ein	Ein	Eine

When a word refers to a person, the gender typically matches the biological gender; however, there is rarely any logic to it for other nouns:

der Vater	die Mutter	das Auto	der Tisch	die Feder
The father	The mother	The car	The table	The feather

For purposes of declension, the plural article for all three is '*die*', and you can consider it to be a fourth gender. German nouns can be pluralized in six different ways, and three of these can also add an umlaut, making a total of nine forms:

	SINGULAR	PLURAL
No ending (with Umlaut)	das Messer (knife)	die Messer
Added E (with Umlaut)	die Wurst (sausage)	die W**ü**rste
Added (E)N	der Hase (rabbit)	die Has**en**
Added ER (with Umlaut)	das Lied (song)	die Lied**er**
Added S	das Büro (office)	die Büro**s**
Irregular	das Datum (date)	die Daten

This all must be too overwhelming for you to learn at once, *keine Sorge!* We have some very simple tips and tricks in our **'Speak German in 30 Days bundle'**, which would help you in remembering the articles of the words. Also, you have been doing *Super* so far!

- Every noun that ends in *-or, -ling, -ig, -ner, or -smus* is masculine and needs to be prefixed by '*Der*'. For instance, you might say: *der Deal, der Huf, der Champion, der Honig, und der Rentner.*

- A noun should be prefixed with the word '*Die*' if it ends in one of the following feminine suffixes: *-ung, -ie, -ei, -keit, heit, schaft, -tät, -ik, or -tion.* For instance, you would say: *die Chance, die Nebenbuhlerin, die Bäckerei, die Blume, die Schönheit, die Bluse, die Universität, die Musik und die Situation.*

- '*Das*' should be used as a prefix to any noun that ends in *-chen, -lein, -ment, -tum, -ma, or -um* if it is neuter. Saying das Mädchen, das Fräulein, das Supplement, das Rittertum, das Schema, and das Museum are a few examples.

We have made a list of some of the most common words used in German with their articles for you, *Lasst uns das lesen!*

ENGLISH	GERMAN
Mother	*die Mutter*
father	*der Vater*
sister	*die Schwester*
brother	*der Bruder*
child	*das Kind*
aunt	*die Tante*
uncle	*der Onkel*
grandmother	*die Großmutter*
grandfather	*der Großvater*
female cousin	*die Cousine*
male cousin:	*der Cousin*
boyfriend	*der Freund*
girlfriend	*die Freundin*
husband	*der Mann*
wife	*die Frau*
male colleague	*der Kollege*
female colleague	*die Kollegin*
male partner	*der Partner*
female partner	*die Partnerin*
house	*das Haus*
bed	*das Bett*
pillow/cushion	*das Kissen*
window	*das Fenster*
wall	*die Wand*
floor	*der Boden*

bedroom	*das Schlafzimmer*
bathroom	*das Badezimmer*
table	*der Tisch*
kitchen	*die Küche*
door	*die Tür*
living room	*die Wohnung*
basement	*der Keller*
couch	*die Couch*
chair	*der Stuhl*
cabinet	*das Kabinett*
dishwasher	*die Geschirrspülmaschine*
microwave	*der Mikrowellenherd*
stove	*der Herd*
refrigerator	*der Kühlschrank*
lamp	*die Lampe*
shower	*die Dusche*
trash	*der Müll*
bathtub	*die Badewanne*
toilet	*die Toilette*
sink	*das Waschbecken*
train	*der Zug*
truck	*der Lastkraftwagen (LKW)*
semi truck	*der Sattelzug*
pass	*der Pass*
ticket	*das Ticket*
school bus	*der Schulbus*

taxi	*das Taxi*
boat	*das Boot*
plane	*das Flugzeug*
bus	*der Bus*
car	*das Auto*
homeland	*das Heimatland*
work	*die Arbeit*
city	*die Stadt*
desert	*die Wüste*
plains	*die Ebenen*
mountain	*der Berg*
country	*das Land*
school	*die Schule*
bread	*das Brot*
breakfast	*das Frühstuck*
milk	*die Milch*
flour	*das Mehl*
snack	*der Snack*
dessert	*das Dessert*
cake	*der Kuchen*
lunch	*das Mittagessen*
egg	*das Ei*
sugar	*der Zucker*
meat	*das Fleisch*
tofu	*der Tofu*
chicken	*das Huhn*

pork	*das Schweinefleisch*
turkey	*der Truthahn*
chocolate	*die Schokolade*
rice	*der Reis*
pancakes	*die Pfannkuchen*
oatmeal	*die Haferflocken*
cereal	*das Müsli*
cracker	*die Cracker*
pizza	*die Pizza*
salad	*der Salat*
dinner	*das Abendessen*
fries	*die Pommes*
spaghetti	*die Spaghetti*
peanut butter	*die Erdnussbutter*
jelly	*das Gelee*
peach	*der Pfirsich*
nut	*die Nuss*
ham	*der Schinken*
pasta	*die Pasta*
burrito	*der Burrito*
zucchini	*die Zucchini*
cucumber	*die Gurke*
onion	*die Zwiebel*
brussel sprouts	*der Rosenkohl*
celery	*der Sellerie*
potato	*die Kartoffel*

broccoli	*der Brokkoli*
tomato	*die Tomate*
lasagna	*die Lasagna*
beans	*die Bohnen*
fish	*der Fisch*
soup	*die Suppe*
burger	*der Burger*
sandwich	*das Sandwich*
macaroni	*die Makkaroni*
banana	*die Banane*
pear	*die Birne*
carrot	*die Karotte*
apple	*der Apfel*
vegetable	*das Gemüse*
fruit	*das Obst*

We have tried to assemble a list of all the basic words and **Wortschatz** which we use in our **Alltagsleben.**

ACHTUNG!!

We learn der die das paired with nouns because der die das is how you say 'the' in the nominative case. Of the 4 German cases, the nominative is the most basic, neutral, and standard.

Aktivitäten:

Solve these basic exercises and train your brain with us!

1. Write the correct articles for the given words with der, die or das:

- _____ Katze
- _____ Pulli
- _____ Hose
- _____ Haus
- _____ Lehrer
- _____ Vater
- _____ Monat
- _____ Tag
- _____ Person
- _____ Maschine
- _____ Jahr
- _____ Nachbarin
- _____ Umwelt
- _____ Stadt
- _____ Heft
- _____ Lippenstift
- _____ Handy
- _____ Kuhlschrank
- _____ Hemd
- _____ Tisch
- _____ Autor
- _____ Schwester
- _____ Rock
- _____ Kleid
- _____ Buch

2. Fill in the blanks with ein/eine:

- _____ Vater

- _____ Hose
- _____ Tag
- _____ Ei
- _____ Person
- _____ Maschine
- _____ Jahr
- _____ Nachbarin
- _____ Umwelt
- _____ Birne
- _____ Heft
- _____ Lippenstift
- _____ Handy
- _____ Kühlschrank
- _____ Schokolade
- _____ Tisch
- _____ Kuli

3. **Fill in the blanks with the words mentioned.**

Sie, Freut mich, heiße, Gute, Guten, geht, spreche, geht's, heißen, Bis

- _____ Nacht.
- Mir _____ es gut.
- Sprechen _____ Englisch?
- _____ später.
- Wie _____ ?
- Ich _____ Marie.
- _____ Sie kennenzulernen.
- Wie _____ Sie?
- Ich _____ kein Deutsch.

- _____Morgen.

4. *Lesen Sie* this story in German and highlight all the words with articles and also find out the greetings mentioned. Try to read it aloud to enhance your pronunciation skills.

Henry Hühnchen

Henry Hühnchen lebt in einem ganz normalen kleinen Hühnerhaus in einem ganz normalen Dorf. Er ist weder groß noch klein. Er ist weder dick noch dünn. Er ist weder schlau noch dumm. Henry Hühnchen ist ein ganz normales Huhn. An einem ganz normalen Morgen isst Henry Hühnchen in der Küche sein Frühstück. Er mag Toast mit Butter und Kaffee mit Sahne. Er liest die Nachrichten im Internet.

Dort sieht er eine furchtbare Nachricht mit einer furchtbaren Überschrift. Sie lautet: 'Der Himmel stürzt ein!' Henry hat so viel Angst, dass er seinen Toast in den Kaffee fallen lässt. Platsch! Der Himmel stürzt ein! 'DER HIMMEL STÜRZT EIN!', ruft Henry. 'Ich muss alle warnen'.

Als erstes schickt er eine E-Mail an seine tausend engsten Freunde. Dann rennt er die Straße hinunter, um alle anderen zu warnen. Die erste Person, die er auf der Straße trifft, ist Hanni Henne. Sie kommt aus dem Supermarkt. 'Guten Morgen, Henry Hühnchen!', sagt Hanni Henne. 'Wohin gehst du? Warum schaust du so ängstlich?

'Der Himmel stürzt ein! Der Himmel stürzt ein!', sagt Henry Hühnchen. Echt? 'Woher weißt du das?', fragt Hanni Henne. 'Ich habe es im Internet gesehen!', sagt Henry Hühnchen. 'Heiliger Bimbam! Dann muss es ja stimmen!', sagt Hanni. 'Los, gehen wir!'

Also rennen Henry Hühnchen und Hanni Henne zusammen die Straße hinunter zum Teich. Als sie am Teich ankommen, treffen sie Erna Ente. Sie badet gerade.

'Hallo, ihr zwei!', sagt Erna Ente. 'Wo geht ihr hin? Warum schaut ihr so ängstlich?' 'Der Himmel stürzt ein! Der Himmel stürzt ein!', rufen Henry Hühnchen und Hanni Henne im Chor. 'Echt? 'Woher wisst ihr das?', fragt Erna Ente.

'Ich habe es im Internet gesehen!', sagt Henry Hühnchen. 'Oh nein! Dann muss es ja stimmen!', sagt Erna. 'Los, gehen wir!' Also rennen Henry Hühnchen, Hanni Henne und Erna Ente die Straße hinunter zum Bauernhof.

Als sie am Bauernhof ankommen, treffen sie Gerda Gans. Sie liest Thea Taube Gedichte vor. 'Hallo zusammen!', sagt Gerda Gans. 'Wo geht ihr hin? Warum schaut ihr so ängstlich?' 'Der Himmel stürzt ein! Der Himmel stürzt ein!', rufen alle zusammen. 'Echt? Woher wisst ihr das?', fragt Thea Taube. 'Wir haben es im Internet gesehen!', rufen alle zusammen.

'Grundgütiger! Dann muss es ja stimmen!', sagt Gerda. 'Wir haben keine Zeit, Gedichte zu lesen. Los, gehen wir!'

Hausaufgabe: make a list of all the German phrases and words mentioned in the Kapitel and write down their meanings!

Ach, endlich! If this is your first time learning and reading the German language, you may be feeling like giving up but we will not let you do that. Well, here's a fact: few people are fluent in German **Artikel**. They will naturally come to you when you are in flow of the language. Even some native speakers may get them wrong on occasion.

In Kapitel 4, we will discuss the basic formation of German sentences, the most commonly used German verbs and also the conjugations of those verbs!
Sind Sie aufgeregt? Because we are!

We are here to help you master the German language with the help of our **'Learn German in 30 days bundle'** and we will make sure that you are **Perfekt** at it.

Bis bald! Alles Gute!

KEY TAKEAWAYS!

In this chapter, we covered the following topics:
- *German's nouns, greetings, and articles of the language.*
- *An introduction to nouns and an explanation of how they function.*

- *Gender distinctions in the German language.*
- *Many common German greetings, including their translations into English, as well as a pronunciation guide to help you pronounce them correctly.*
- *A collection of articles written in German, each with an accompanying explanation.*
- *The guidelines and strategies for learning the German articles in their appropriate order.*
- *A rundown of all the essential words in the German language, along with their definitions and the articles that go with them.*
- *A little narrative to help with both your pronunciation and your overall knowledge of the German language.*
- *Shortened form of the traditional German greetings.*
- *How and where to greet people in various settings according to the circumstances.*

ANTWORTEN! ANSWER KEY

1. ((page 60)
- Tschüss
- Guten Tag
- Mahlzeit
- Wie geht's?

2. (Page 60)
- GUTEN TAG
- GUTEN ABEND
- GUTE NACHT
- HALLO
- WIE GEHT'S
- VIELLEICHT
- ODER
- ABER
- ENTSCHULDIGUNG

3. (page 72)
- Gute
- geht
- Sie

- Bis
- geht's
- heiße
- Freut mich
- heißen
- spreche
- Guten

KAPITEL 4

Übung ist der beste Lehrmeister - Lateinisches Sprichwort

Hallo zusammen, Wie geht es Ihnen?

Herzlich willkommen zum Kapitel 4!

Hallo! As we know, practice makes perfect (*Übung macht den meister*) Mastering German sentence form is the only path to fluency. If you want to write better sentences, you need to know which rules to follow. But don't worry, we are here to help you with our '**Learn German in 30 days bundle**'. Imagine you are in Germany on a vacation and want to make new friends, but having a conversation with someone requires an understanding of basic sentence construction before you can move on to more complex topics like world affairs, right? In **Kapitel 4**, we will help you out with that!

To help you out, we have collected all the *wichtige* guidelines for German sentence construction. Sentence construction in German is notoriously challenging for students just starting out, so let us assist you. Never again will you have to wonder if you're using the correct word order in German. First things first, let's learn how to use the personal pronouns in German and their conjugations! *So, Los gehts!*

GERMAN PERSONAL PRONOUNS

German pronouns are also a sentence's building block, just like in English. In German, pronouns are known as *pronomen (pro-nom-en)*. When compared to English pronouns, they are a little more complex but we will make them easier for you in our '**Learn German in 30 days bundle**' as we always do!

Let's start by comparing the English and German languages. First off, English has no other term for 'you' in a formal context. German, however, uses two distinct words.

- Informal you is *'du'*, and formal you is *'Sie'* which is always capitalized.
- Second, the accusative and dative cases in German have different pronouns, whereas in English, in both circumstances, pronouns remain the same.

Fangen wir an? 1..2..3..Los geht's!

Wir is also a *pronomen* in German which means 'we', what is the case? Well, we will also help you understand the German cases soon. Let's start with the basics now, what are pronouns?

A word that is used in placc of a noun is called a pronoun. The explanation is simple and clear: it does not appear to be proper to use the same noun in a series of different contexts. The use of appropriate pronouns can significantly improve the readability of a sentence.

Zum Beispiel: Peter bought a new house and he loves it. 'He' refers to Peter in this sentence, and the new house is the subject.

Pronouns such as *he, she, I, you, me, it, we, they, myself, and yourself* are examples of common English pronouns. They differ not only in gender and number, but also according to the case of the words.

Zum Beispiel: I presented him with the book. At this point, the subject switches from 'he' to 'him', making him the indirect object.

German Personal Pronouns

In place of nouns, we use several personal pronouns or *Personal pronomen*. A noun can refer to a particular person, location, or object in the world. These pronouns are used when we want to talk about the previously mentioned nouns.

In addition to addressing other people, we might communicate about ourselves when we use these. Have a look at the given table to understand them more:

		Nominativ	Akkusativ	Dativ
Singular	1st person	ich	mich	mir

	2nd person	du	dich	dir
	3rd person	Er, sie, es	ihn, sie, es	ihm, ihr, ihn
Plural	1st person	wir	uns	uns
	2nd person	ihr	euch	euch
	3rd person	sie, Sie	sie, Sie	ihnen, Ihnen

Lets also see how to use these with the help of some examples:

- **Ich** *lese ein Buch. Es ist sehr interessant.* (I am reading a book. It is interesting.)
- *Peter geht mit **ihr** ins Theater.* (Peter is going to the theater with her.)
- *Wie geht es **dir** heute?* (How are you today?)

If you feel as though you have a general understanding of what has been discussed so far, you are likely prepared to go on to the next subject.

There, we will discuss the questions that need to be answered before we can apply personal pronouns to your German.

- *Which person is the noun in?*
- *In what case does the noun appear?*
- *In the event that the noun refers to an object, what gender would it be?*

Possessive pronouns are used when we want to indicate that something belongs to someone. In short, these pronouns indicate possession. They are:

- *ich* – mein (my)
- *du* – dein (your)
- *er* – sein (his)
- *sie* – ihr (her)
- *es* – sein (its)
- *wir* – unser (our)
- *ihr* – euer (your)

- *sie* – ihr (their)
- *Sie* – Ihr (your)

In most cases, possessive pronouns appear before the nouns they refer to. As a result of this, they are also referred to as possessive articles.

Even more so than regular articles, these pronouns have a variety of endings that depend on the gender, number of people being referred to, and case.

Consider the use of the pronoun *mein* as an example. The declension of it is as described in the table given below:

	Maskuline	Feminine	Neutral	Plural
Nominativ	mein	mein**e**	mein	mein**e**
Accusative	mein**en**	mein**e**	mein	mein**e**
Dative	mein**em**	mein**er**	mein**em**	mein**en** + n
Genitive	mein**es**	mein**er**	mein**es**	mein**er**

Zum beispiel:

- Das ist **mein** Kuli. (That is my pen.)
- Er ist der Sohn **meines** Freundes. (He is my friend's son.)
- Er hat **seine** Flasche vergessen. (He forgot his bottle.)

Aktivität:

1. **Write the appropriate personal pronouns in the given sentences:**

- _____ bist pünktlich.
- _____ sind pünktlich.
- _____ ist aus Deutschland.
- _____ seid in Spanien.

- _____ sind in Spanien.
- _____ kauft eine Zeitung. _____ ist von heute.
- Mia hat einen neuen Tisch. _____ ist braun.

2. Fill in the blanks with the appropriate personal pronoun, make sure that it is conjugated right:

- Der Student fragt den Professor: 'Herr Professor Schmidt _____ Sie morgen Zeit für ein Gespräch über meine Dissertation?'

- Ich liebe meine neue Sonnenbrille, _____ sieht so schick aus.

- Oma, Opa und ich gehen morgen in die Oper. _____ hören gerne klassische Musik.

- Paul fragt seinen Schulfreund Peter: _____ mir bitte deinen Pullover geben? Mir ist so kalt.'

- Katzen sind besonders intelligente Tiere und _____ sind auch sehr emotional.

- Meine neue Küche ist hochmodern und _____ bietet Luxus und Komfort.

- Der Patient fragt den Doktor: 'Herr Doktor haben _____ kein stärkeres Medikament gegen meine Schmerzen?'

- Hannes und Jutta, _____ seid beide 10 Jahre alt, nicht?

- Ich finde Danielas neuen Hut sehr extravagant. _____ ist mir etwas zu farbenfroh.

- Mama, _____ mir bei meinen Hausübungen helfen?

- Das Auto meines Nachbarn hat eine tolle Farbe. _____ ist gelb wie eine Zitrone.

- Opa und Oma, warum habt _____ wieder so viel gekocht? Wir sind doch nur drei Leute.

The Functions of Nouns Within a Sentence

First, let's take a look at how to determine the function that a noun serves in a particular sentence. Right now, there are three primary roles that require our attention: *the subject, the direct object, and the indirect object.*

No matter what function a noun serves, it must always be placed in the case that corresponds to that function. For instance, if the noun in question is the subject of the sentence, you must use the *nominative case* for it.

Case	Role	Action performed
Nominative	Subject	Takes action
Accusative	Direct object	Receives action
Dative	Indirect object	to/for whom action is taken
Genitive	possessive	Indicates ownership of something/someone

ACHTUNG!!

In English, we do not typically differentiate between direct and indirect objects; rather, we refer to all things that are objects as simply objects.

On the other hand, the distinction between the accusative case and the dative case is still quite important in German.

We have already given a table of all the cases above and you can see how the gender of the noun also affects the ending and helps us decide which case to use correctly. We hope this has been enjoyable for you so far, *Ja? Gut!* Now let's move on to the basic sentence structure of the German language!!

GERMAN SENTENCE STRUCTURE

Let's start with the fundamentals: main clauses and verbs.

Main clauses are the building blocks of a sentence and are sometimes referred to as *'independent clauses'* or *'declarative sentences'* (**Hauptsätze/Aussagesätze**). With a subject, a verb, and an object, at the very least, these sentences convey an entire idea.

The verb is the heart of the sentence. These words, which are often called *'action words,'* explain what has happened, is happening, or will happen.

Whether in the past, the present, or the future, verbs can also represent a situation. Every sentence needs a verb in order to make sense. But how do we write German, what is the order of German sentences?

You can use the same word order as in English when writing a simple main sentence in German. Lets see with this *Beispiel*:

I <u>gave</u> the boy a ball, how do we write this sentence in German?
Well, easy:

'Ich <u>gab</u> dem Jungen einen Ball'

Now, what is the structure of this sentence? The **subject-verb-object** structure of simple declarative sentences in English can be applied to German grammar as well and this is shown with the above given example.

Yet, we can alter the word order of sentences in German to emphasize certain points because the four cases enable us to determine whether a noun or pronoun is being used as a subject or an object.

The subject **Ich** is in the first place and the verb **gab** is in the second place which is followed by the object **ball**, what does *gab* mean anyway? Well, **Gab** is a conjugated form of the word *'geben'* and *geben* means <u>to give</u>.

Always remember, the verb always remains in <u>second place</u> in the German language, the verb has to be conjugated and you will learn about all the basic verbs and their conjugations in our **'Learn German in 30 days bundle'**.

SOME BASIC RULES FOR GERMAN SENTENCE FORMATION:

The following are the key rules for proper word order:

- In every sentence, the second spot on the line is dedicated to the finite verb.
- Forms of the verb that can be extended indefinitely, such as infinitives and past participles, are used at the end of the sentence.
- The subject of the sentence is often positioned at the beginning of the sentence the majority of the time. **Warum?** In German, it is possible for other parts of the phrase, such as the object, the place, or the time, to come before the beginning of the sentence. Because of this, the subject is placed after the finite verb in the sentence.
- The majority of the time, the following structure should be followed to construct a sentence in the correct order:

1st position		finite verb	subject	indirect object	time	place	direct object	infinite verb
subject	*Der Lehrer*	*hat*		*dem Schüler*	*gestern*	*in der Schule*	*den Test*	*zurück-gegeben.*
indirect object	*Dem Schüler*	*hat*	*der Lehrer*		*gestern*	*in der Schule*	*den Test*	*zurück-gegeben.*
direct object	*Den Test*	*hat*	*der Lehrer*	*dem Schüler*	*gestern*	*in der Schule*		*zurück-gegeben.*
time	*Gestern*	*hat*	*der Lehrer*	*dem Schüler*		*in der Schule*	*den Test*	*zurück-gegeben.*
place	*In der Schule*	*hat*	*der Lehrer*	*dem Schüler*	*gestern*		*den Test*	*zurück-gegeben.*

The structure of sentences in German can vary significantly depending on a wide variety of factors. In spite of the fact that German verbs often come after the subject, it is allowed in some contexts to switch the order of the clauses in a sentence.

This is something that we can do for a variety of purposes, including determining where the attention should be placed. The clause or phrase that we wish to highlight is moved to the front of the sentence, where it is then followed by the verb in its many conjugations, and then the subject and the remainder of the sentence are brought to a conclusion.

We will use some examples to show how you can rearrange German sentences in a variety of ways. The first statement, '***Die Katze isst das Essen des Hundes,***' ('The cat eats the food of the dog.') can also be written also be written in the following word order:

- *Des Hundes Essen isst die Katze.*
- The dog's food eats the cat.

- *Das Essen des Hundes isst die Katze.*
- The food of the dog eats the cat.

- *Die Katze isst des Hundes Essen.*
- The cat eats the dog's food.

We made an effort to maintain the original German sentence's word order in the English translations given. Clearly, only the last sentence makes any sense in English, although all three are appropriate in German.

Don't give up, we are sure that with some simple tips and tricks followed by practice exercises would make you a master of the German sentence structure!

ACHTUNG!!

Whenever the pronoun serving as the direct object is also a noun, it comes before the indirect object.

example: der Test = ihn

'Der Lehrer hat ihn dem Schüler gestern in der Schule zurückgegeben.'

A separable prefix, such as *'am-,'* *'um-,'* or *'Aber-,'* is added at the end of the sentence if the verb in question has one.

'Wir verlassen den Raum', for instance, is a short statement that simply says 'We leave the room.' *'Ich werfe den Müll weg,'* or 'I dispose of the garbage,' is another example of a detachable prefix.

In this sentence, the prefix *'weg-'* from the verb 'wegwerfen' has been moved to the end of the sentence, **Klar? Nein? Kein Problem!**

TWO VERBS IN GERMAN SENTENCES

Using two verbs in a single sentence is not uncommon in German. It's important for you to learn how it functions in a sentence, whether you're speaking in the past tense or have a very complicated thought. It's actually quite simple, and we will make it even simpler for you!

Among your verbs, one will stand out as the main one or the dominant one. With the past tense, you would say **'haben'** (to have). The most important verb comes first in German. Here is the one where conjugation is used. The secondary verb might be left in its infinitive form or conjugated into the past tense according to standard practice. Then, move the second verb to the end of the sentence. Even if it comes at the conclusion of the sentence and isn't explicitly conjugated, that's the verb that gives your sentence its meaning, therefore it's still the primary verb. Let's look at a few examples and make it even easier to understand for you:

- I have rented a bicycle. – *Ich <u>habe</u> ein Rad gemietet.*
- You must take a detour. – *Sie <u>müssen</u> einen Umweg machen.*
- Mr. Meier can help you. – *Herr Meier <u>kann</u> Ihnen helfen.*

<u>Aktivität</u>: **try to find out the <u>secondary</u> verbs used in the above sentences and also write down their meaning!**

Different German Conjunctions and How to Use this Them in Sentences

German conjunctions are a core part of the German language, just like they are in English or any other language. Do the sentences below share any connections with one another?

*'He was exhausted after the long meeting **and** he fell asleep in a minute.'*

*'I want to watch the movie, **but** I need to sleep right now.'*

Indeed, there is a connection! Words like **and** or **but** link the two sentences together. These words are referred to as *conjunctions*. The proper use of several German conjunctions in sentences and their implications on word order will help you to understand the language and the sentence structure better.

Types of German Conjunctions

German conjunctions are the words that link two sentences, as was mentioned earlier. Without them, the sentences would be short and creating complex statements and sentences would be extremely challenging to create. It's essential that you know when to use each conjunction in order to successfully convey your ideas and views.

Subordinating conjunctions, coordinating conjunctions, and two-part or compound conjunctions are the three forms of conjunctions used in English.

Conjunctions that are subordinate have an impact on sentence structure. You will learn everything there is to know about German compounds and coordinate conjunctions now. ***Fangen wir an!***

Coordinating Conjunctions in German

German coordinating conjunctions join two separate clauses or key clauses. They have no impact on where the verb is placed. As a result, the sentence structure is identical to that of a typical independent clause. The verb will be in the second place after being conjugated.

These German conjunctions do not influence the word order, to summarize it. The words will be arranged as follows:

Complex sentence = Main clause 1 + Main clause 2

Main clause 2 = Coordinating conjunction + Subject + Conjugated verb + ...

The conjunction is considered to be in the zero position, as seen above (*Nullposition*). Thus, the first position subject is followed by the conjugated verb (second position).

Now, you will have to learn about the most frequently used coordinate conjunctions, the easiest way is to learn them by heart, but they will start to come automatically to you as you practice more!

Look at this provided table of the most important coordinate conjunctions:

GERMAN	ENGLISH
aber	but
denn	because
sondern	but / but rather
oder	or
doch / jedoch	however
beziehungsweise	or precisely
und	and

Let's try to imply these in simple sentences to give you an idea:

- *Die Sonne scheint **und** die Vögel singen.*
  The sun is shining and the birds are singing.

- *Das Wohnzimmer ist schön, **aber** zu dunkel.*
  The living room is lovely, but too dark.

- *Sie muss sich ausruhen, **denn** sie ist krank.*
  She must rest because she is ill.

- *Ich singe nicht gern, **sondern** tanze sehr gerne.*

  I don't like to sing, but I like to dance.

We hope these examples will clear your doubts!

Aktivitat:

1. **Write sentences using the given connectors:**

- Aber _____

- Denn _____

- Weil _____

- Sondern _____

- Oder _____

- Und _____

- Beziehungsweise _____

- Doch _____

2. **Write the missing connectors, you can use the connectors given below:**
   Aber, weil, oder, denn

- Ich muss arbeiten, _____ ich muss auch das Abendessen kochen.

- Ich muss heute zu einer Besprechung gehen, _____ das Büro geöffnet ist.

- Ich würde gerne etwas unternehmen, _____ ich muss Hausaufgaben machen.

- Was möchten Sie, gelb_____ blau?

- Das Wetter ist gut, _____ ich kann keinen Urlaub nehmen.

- Alle Kinder werden gebeten, in Uniform zu erscheinen, _____ wir werden heute das Klassenfoto machen.

Subordinate Clause

Subordinate clauses are integrated into the main phrase with the help of subordinating conjunctions in German. The proper word order for a subordinate clause is the subordinating conjunction followed by the subject of the sentence and the conjugated verb.

The verb follows the ending of the subordinate clause in such examples. You can put subordinate clauses at the beginning or the conclusion of a sentence, just like in English, so long as the sentence has at least one independent clause. This is necessary because without it the sentence would be a fragment. ***Zum beispiel:***

- ***Ich trinke, weil du mich verlassen <u>hast</u>.***
- I'm drinking because you left me.

The conjunction ***'weil'*** connects the two clauses. Such conjunctions are known as **subordinate conjunctions.**

Subordinate Conjunctions in German

As the name implies, subordinate conjunctions are used to join dependent clauses to their main clauses. In certain cases, they may also be called subjunctions. Subordinate conjunctions are used to introduce subordinate clauses in German sentences.

The German language has a broad variety of subordinating conjunctions. Having a working knowledge of all of them is essential, as they are constantly being used in conversation.

The only way to do this successfully, is to memorize them. So there's no reason to worry, we have compiled a list for you. As you use them more frequently, they will become easy for you and you will be able to use the correct one every time! *Ok, gut!*

These are the most essential and most often used subordinate conjunctions in German:

German	English
dass	that
bevor	before
bis	until
wenn	if / whenever
weil	because
während	during / while
sowie	as well as / as soon as
soweit	as far as
sodass	so that
nachdem	after
indem	while
ob	whether / if
falls	in case
als	as / when
damit	so that
seit	since
obwohl	although
sobald	as soon as

As long as one sticks to the basic rules of the sentence formations, German sentence construction is quite easy and easy to grasp.

ACHTUNG!!

Compound Sentence = Main Clause + Subordinate Clause

Aktivität:

1. **Read the following excerpt taken from a short story in German, underline the verbs given and identify their positions, also recognize the different types of verbs used and the sentence structure:**

Die Drei Kleinen Schweinchen

Es war einmal eine Schweinemutter, die hatte drei kleine Schweinchen. Sie hat sie sehr geliebt, aber es war nicht genug Essen für alle da, also hat sie sie in die Welt geschickt, um ihr eigenes Glück zu suchen.

Das erste kleine Schweinchen beschloss, in den Süden zu gehen. Als er die Straße entlang lief, traf er einen Bauern, der ein Bündel Stroh trug, also fragte er den Mann freundlich: 'Können Sie mir bitte das Stroh geben, damit ich mir ein Haus bauen kann?' Weil das kleine Schweinchen 'bitte' sagte, gab der Bauer ihm das Stroh und das kleine Schweinchen baute daraus ein schönes Haus. Das Haus hatte Strohwände, einen Strohboden und innen... ein bequemes Strohbett.

Gerade als das kleine Schweinchen mit dem Hausbau fertig war und sich für ein Nickerchen in sein Strohbett legte, kam der große böse Wolf zu dem Haus. Er roch das Schweinchen in dem Haus und ihm lief das Wasser im Mund zusammen. 'Mmmmm... Brot mit Speck!'

Also klopfte der Wolf an die Tür des Strohhauses und sagte: 'Kleines Schwein! Kleines Schwein! Lass mich herein! Lass mich herein!'

Aber das kleine Schweinchen sah die großen Pfoten des Wolfes durch das Schlüsselloch und antwortete: 'Nein! Nein! Nein! Ich lass dich nicht herein!'

Dann zeigte der Wolf seine Zähne und sagte: 'Ich werde husten und prusten und dir dein Haus zusammen pusten!' Also hustete und prustete er und pustete das Haus zusammen und das kleine Schweinchen rannte zurück nach Hause zu seiner Mutter.

Das zweite kleine Schweinchen beschloss, in den Norden zu gehen. Als er die Straße entlang lief, traf er einen Bauern, der ein Bündel Holz trug, also fragte er den Mann freundlich: 'Entschuldigen Sie, kann ich das Holz haben, um ein Haus zu bauen?'

2. **Write the meanings of the given words from the excerpt, also identify the verb conjugations wherever necessary:**

   - Hatte
   - Gelieben
   - Geschickten
   - Beschloss
   - Klopfen
   - Holzhaus
   - Schwein
   - Mutter
   - Böse
   - Weil
   - Klein
   - Pusten
   - Speck
   - Brot
   - Süd
   - Essen
   - Treffen
   - Holzwand
   - Zähne
   - Bauen
   - Liefen
   - Tragen
   - Antworten
   - Bitte
   - Straße

- Entschuldigung
- Können
- Strohbett
- Fertig
- Husten
- Stellen
- Machen
- Geben
- Glück
- Blumen
- Tragen
- Daraus
- Herein
- Prusten
- Bequem
- Große
- Mag
- Freundlich
- Zusammen
- Zeigen
- Schön
- Genug

How Should Dependent Clauses Be Used to Construct Sentences in German?

German always uses a comma to divide its major clauses from its dependent clauses, in contrast to English. Also, as we have already discussed above that subordinate conjunctions always come first in German subordinate clauses.

Hence, the conjugated verb is always placed at the end of the subordinate sentence, and this is the most important rule to remember. The verb's place within the main clause does not change when the sentence begins with it.

Zum Beispiel: *Ich weiß nicht, ob er heute zur Party kommt.* (I don't know if he is coming to the party today.)

Here, the key sentence is *Ich weiß nicht*. The subordinate clause is *Er kommt heute zur Party*. A **comma (,)** separates these two phrases, and the subjunctive **ob** joins them.

ACHTUNG!!

Subordinate clause =

Subordinate conjunction + Subject + … + Conjugated Verb

Main Clause after Subordinate Clause

In German, the order of these two clauses is <u>interchangeable</u>. This indicates that the subordinate clause may appear before the main clause in the sentence.

Zum Beispiel: *Bevor er das Haus verlässt,* <u>**trinkt**</u> *er immer Kaffee.* (Before he leaves the house, he always drinks coffee.)

You must have observed that there have been some changes made to the main clause. Just after the comma, that is, before the subject, comes the verb, which is often in the second position. But what about all those words before the verb, the verb has to be in second position, right? What if we tell you that in the given **Beispiel** the verb is placed correctly, that is, in its second position. Don't get overwhelmed and confused, there is a very easy explanation for this!

You are all familiar with the German word order. Whether the statement is simple or complex, the verb is always in the second position. The <u>entire subordinate clause is regarded as being in the first position</u> in the example above. The main clause's verb is placed before the subject so that it keeps its second position.

Now does that make sense? We told you, German is not as complicated as you think it is, and with our **'Learn German in 30 days bundle',** you will understand all the key concepts in 30 days!

ACHTUNG!!

Complex sentence =

Subordinate clause (position 1) + Verb (position 2) + Subject + Rest of the sentence

German Subordinate Clauses and Verb Forms

There are two verbs in a sentence when using modal verbs, perfect tense, or passive voice. What are modal verbs, is this your next question? Don't worry, we will get to modal verbs very soon.

First just remember that the conjugated verb is placed at the end of the clause in accordance with the same rules as in others, _zum Beispiel:_

- _Du <u>musst</u> studieren, wenn du die Prüfung bestehen <u>willst</u>._ (You have to study if you want to pass the exam.)
- _Ich <u>habe</u> den Bus verpasst, weil ich spät aufgewacht <u>bin</u>._ (I missed the bus because I woke up late.)

The conjugated verbs **willst** and **bin** are present at the end of the sentence, as can be seen in the examples above. Separable verbs also fall under the same condition. The separable prefix is no longer separated since the conjugated verb is now placed at the end. The conjugated verb and prefix are written as a single word.

Zum Beispiel:

Ich kann nicht sofort kommen, weil ich immer noch mein Zimmer aufräume. (I cannot come right away because I am still cleaning up my room.)

The Structure of Questions in German (W Fragen) _(way-fraag-en)_

What are question words in German? Again, the form of the sentence changes very little from English to German when you're asking a question in German.

To clarify, if a question has two verbs, the first verb must be conjugated, and the second verb must be placed at the end of the question. Yet, there are question words in German, just like there are in English. Because all of these words begin with a 'w,' they are collectively referred to as W-Worter in German. Everything that starts with a 'W' is a question in German, some of these are:

- why – *warum*
- what – *was*
- when – *wann*
- how – *wie*
- where – *wo*
- where from – *woher*
- where to – *wohin*
- who – *wer*
- who(m) – *wen*
- whose – *wessen*
- to/from whom – *wem*

In German, forming a question can be done in either of two ways. Either a word that indicates a question is used, or the word order might be switched around. As you can see in the table that is located above, all of the German question words start with the letter W, which is why they are referred to as W-Fragen.

The following is a list of some other often used question words:

Since when	*Seit wann*
With whom	*Mit wem*
Whose	*Wessen*
Is there	*Gibt es*
How many	*Wie viele*
How much	*Wie viel*
How long	*Wie lange*

Some examples of German *Fragen sind*:

- Can I rent a car here? – *Kann ich hier ein Auto mieten?*
- When did you arrive? – *Wann sind Sie angekommen?*

Aktivität:

1. **Write down the suitable word for the given questions. Fill in the blanks!**

- _____ ist die Telefonnummer von Petra?
- _____ arbeiten Sie auch am Wochenende?
- _____ fährt er in den Urlaub? - Nach Berlin.
- _____ macht er in der Freizeit?
- _____ ist die Schule deiner Tochter?
- _____ gehen wir in den Supermarkt?
- _____ kommen alle Tänzer und Sänger?
- _____ es hier einen Park? - Ja.
- _____ soll die Natur schützen? - Alle Menschen.
- _____ Rock findest du schön?
- _____ machen Sie hier?
- _____ suchen Sie?

Ach, endlich! This was all about the basic cases in German and also the sentence formation, you may be feeling like giving up but we will not let you do that. It's just a little way more, and you will be the master of these in no time. They will naturally come to you when you are in flow of the language. Even some native speakers may get the cases, endings and '*w*' *Fragen* wrong on occasion.

So, don't worry about it too much and just make a *Rateversuch*. Well, half the time what you think is right, would be right, that's how language works, you also have to trust your gut! We hope this was also *spaß, ja? Gut!*

In Kapitel 5, we will discuss the verbs in the German languages, their meanings, conjugations and also learn how to form sentences using them! *Sind Sie aufgeregt?* Because we are!

We are here to help you master the German language with the help of our **'Learn German in 30 days bundle'** and we will make sure that you are *Perfekt* at it.

Bis bald! Alles Gute!

KEY TAKEAWAYS!

Some important points which we covered in this chapter are:

- *The basic sentence formation in the German language*
- *Learning the different German cases and also their declensions.*
- *Learning how to derive the proper form of noun to be used in the sentences.*
- *German personal pronouns, reflexive pronouns and possessive pronouns.*
- *Nominative case with its examples, accusative case with its examples and genitive case with its examples.*
- *The uses and the functions of a pronoun in the German language and sentences.*
- *The most important rules for the formation of the different types of sentence formation*
- *Different German conjugations and how to use them.*
- *Many conjugations like aber, denn, weil, und, oder, denn with their meanings and appropriate way to use them.*
- *'W' Fragen and how to build questions in German language*
- *Subordinate conjunctions*

ANTWORTEN! ANSWER KEY

Pg 84, Q1

Du

Sie

Er

Ihr

Sie

Er, Sie

Er

Pg 85, Q2

haben Sie

Sie

Wir

kannst du

sie

sie

haben Sie

Ihr

Er

kannst du

Es

ihr

Page 95, Q2

Aber

Weil

Aber

Oder

Aber

Denn

Pg 104, Q1

Wie

Warum

Wohin

Was

Wo

Wann

Woher

Gibt

Wer

Welchen

Was

Was

KAPITEL 5

Übe dich nur Tag um Tag und du wirst sehn, was das vermag
von *Johann Wolfgang von Goethe*

Hallo zusammen, Wie geht es Ihnen?

Herzlich willkommen zum Kapitel 5!

Hallo! How was the last *Kapitel* with the sentence formation and rules, we hope you had fun! Well, you are here now and ready to take a deep step into the German language. As we know, practicing German form is the only path to fluency. If you want to write better sentences, you need to know which verbs to use and how to use them correctly. But don't worry, we are here to help you with our '**Learn German in 30 days bundle**'.

There are so many verbs in a language, every action we do, go out, walk, swim, run, eat, everything is important in a language and so verbs also play an important part in the German language. In **Kapitel 5**, we will help you out with the German verbs, their correct conjugations and also talk about the tenses! Are you ready to get started?

Los gehts!

VERBS: WHAT ARE THEY?

The verb is the most essential component of a sentence. They explain the activity that has taken place, is taking place, or is going to take place and are sometimes referred to as action words. Verbs not only express actions, but also states of being, which might be located in the past, the present, or the future. In order for a sentence to be considered full, it must have at least one verb.

You need to first have a solid grasp of tenses and conjugation in German before you can even begin to understand German verbs. But what exactly is conjugation? And how does it matter to us?

The ending of the verb will vary according to when the event took place, who carried it out, and both of those factors combined. This process, known as conjugation, involves changing the ending of an infinitive verb in order to specify the person who carried out an action and the time it took place. Let's take a deeper look into the conjugations and tenses!

CONJUGATIONS

In German, infinitive verbs are those that finish in -en, whereas in English, infinitive verbs require the preposition 'to' before them. For instance, we have the verb 'to kick' (**treten**), as well as the verb 'to run' (**laufen**). Yet, what exactly is an infinitive? We will clear it further for you!

The word 'infinitive' refers to the most basic form of the verb. The word 'to' is included in the infinitive form of the verb in English; for example, 'to live,' 'to read,' and 'to discover.' The infinitives of most German words end in -en, however there are a few exceptions to this rule that result in words ending in -n.

The person or thing doing the action is referred to as the subject of the verb in both German and English. When used with different subjects, verbs always alter their endings, which is a process known as conjugation. In addition, conjugation is determined not only by the tense of the verb but also by the time period in which the event takes place.

So, the conjugation of 'to run' in the present tense third-person singular in English is 'he runs,' whereas in German, the word **'laufen'** is transformed into **'er läuft.'**

Is the concept of conjugation and infinitive clear now? **Ja, sehr gut!**

Now let's also discuss the different tenses in the German language, the German language has six tenses, they are:

- *present (Präsens)*
- *present perfect (Perfekt)*
- *simple past (Präteritum)*

- *past perfect (Plusquamperfekt)*
- *future (Futur I)*
- *future perfect (Futur II)*

But what are Tenses and why are they used? Let's find out!

GERMAN TENSES

The time when something is happening is indicated by the tense. It could be in the present, the past, or the future. The following are the German tenses that are most frequently used:

PRÄSENS (PRESENT TENSE)

The present tense is the first tense that you will study in German. It is used to communicate about things that are happening right now, things that are ongoing, things that often happen or frequently happen, and things that could happen in the near future.

The verb stem determines how to conjugate the present tense, as it does with other tenses. So for now, let's simply concentrate on the tenses, their functions, and a few examples:

- *Ich lerne Deutsch* (I am learning German)
- *Er hat einen Hund* (he has a dog)
- *Sie kommen nicht* (They aren't coming)

The last example is showing us how the present tense can be used to discuss future events.

PERFEKT (PRESENT PERFECT)

When discussing events that happened recently (within the last few minutes, hours, days, weeks, or months), or while speaking casually to someone, the **Perfekt** tense is used in German. This can be done either vocally or in writing, such in an email, for example.

The present tense of the verbs **sein** (to be) or **haben** (to have) and the past participles of these are used to conjugate verbs in the perfect tense. The auxiliary verb, or helping verb, used to create the perfect tense is either **haben** or **sein**. What is past participle, you ask? The verb form known as the past participle indicates a finished activity.

One thing to always remember is that like 'kicked' or 'slept,' these words in English have an ending of -d, -ed, or -t. Similar to German, English has several irregular verbs that you should look out for.

How to make the past participle? Regular German verbs require the addition of **ge-** to the beginning and **-t** to the end to make the past participle. Also, you must add **ge-** to the verb stem's beginning and **-en** to its ending for irregular verbs.

Zum Beispiel:

- *Wir sind nach Amerika gefahren* (We went to America)
- *Ich habe ihm meine Nummer gegeben* (I gave him my phone number)
- *Du hast das ganze Essen gegessen* (You have eaten all the food)

PRÄTERITUM (SIMPLE PAST TENSE)

For any event occurring further in the past or to put it simply, something which has happened long, long ago, the simple past tense, also known as the **Präteritum** or preterit tense in English, is used (years, decades, and centuries ago). It can also be used while speaking to someone in a formal manner.

Now let's understand präteritum with some examples:

- *Mozart zog 1781 nach Wien um* (Mozart moved to Vienna in 1781)
- *Big Ben wurde 1859 fertiggestellt* (Big Ben was completed in 1859)

PLUSQUAMPERFEKT (PAST PERFECT TENSE)

The past perfect tense, sometimes referred to as the pluperfect tense or **Plusquamperfekt**, represents an activity that happened before another action in the past.

Similar to how the present perfect tense is constructed in German, the past perfect tense is also formed, with the exception that the auxiliary (again, either **haben** or **sein**) is in its simple past tense form. There are some examples to help you grasp it better:

- *Der Wolf hatte die Großmutter schon gefressen, als Rotkäppchen ins Haus kam.* (The wolf had already eaten the grandmother before Little Red Riding-Hood came into the house)

- *Wir hatten gut gespielt, bis sie verletzt wurde* (We had played well until she was injured)

FUTUR I (FUTURE TENSE)

When discussing a future occurrence in German, the future tense is similar to the way it is expressed in English when we say 'I/you/he/she/it/we/they will...'

You only need to be familiar with all the conjugations of **werden** (*will*) and then add an infinitive verb to complete the formation of this tense. This makes it one of the simplest tenses to master. Zum beispiel:

- *Wir werden versuchen, langsamer zu essen* (We will try to eat more slowly)
- *Ich werde Ihnen die Antwort sagen* (I will tell you the answer)
- *Gebt und ihr werdet wiederum empfangen* (Give, and you will in turn receive)

FUTUR II (FUTURE PERFECT TENSE)

And finally, we have arrived at our last tense in the discussion: the future perfect tense or **Futur II**. A past participle is as much necessary for this, as it is for the other perfect tenses.

In German, the future perfect is formed by combining the verb **werden** with the appropriate past participle and the verbs **haben** or **sein**.

Once more, this is quite close to the English phrase 'shall have'. The only thing that is different is that, as is standard practise in German, the verb that is not conjugated is moved to the end of the clause, have a look at these examples to understand it better:

- *Wenn ihr ankommt, werden wir ein Hotel gefunden haben.* (By the time you arrive, we will have found a hotel)
- *Bis heute Abend werden wir das Geschirr gespült haben* (By this evening, we will have done the dishes)

MOODS IN GERMAN

Now we will also discuss some of the German moods. In particular, a significant amount of real German speech is composed of the present and perfect tenses, which are respectively referred to as *Prasens* and *Perfekt*. We are sure you have gotten the hang of them by now, eh? The *Prasens* is used for a significant portion of the future in addition to the present, whereas the *Perfekt* is used for practically anything that took place in the past.

The moods are simpler to explain, so let's start with those:

- ***Indikativ*** and indicative are the most common moods in both languages. They are used to describe reality, including things that have actually occurred, are currently occurring, or are anticipated to occur in the future.

- The ***Konjunktiv I*** is used to set the author apart from reported or indirect speech, ***zum Beispiel***: '*according to his manager, he is unaware of the scandal*' It is primarily used in news reporting and has no relevant English counterpart.

- The conditional mood in English is comparable to the ***Konjunktiv II***. It typically employs a form of '*werden*' in the similar way that we use 'would' ('I wouldn't do that' would be '*Ich würde das nicht tun*'), and it expresses hypothetical and/or conditional actions.

- Get away!' and 'Clean your room!' are examples of instructions that use the ***Imperativ***/Imperative mood. Because of the fact that it only occurs in the present tense and in the second person, it is the simplest mood to master in both the languages, English and German. The verb's infinitive form can occasionally be used as an imperative in German.

WEAK, STRONG, AND IRREGULAR VERBS

The pattern of conjugation that a verb follows might determine whether it is considered regular in English. Verbs can be either regular or irregular. There are three categories of verbs in German: weak, powerful, and irregular.

The part of an infinitive form of a verb that is left after removing the ending -***en*** (or -n, in a few circumstances) is referred to as the stem of the verb. In order to conjugate a verb, you must attach the proper ending to the root of the verb, taking into account the subject and the tense. The table that follows provides a list of some of the most typical weak verbs.

GERMAN	ENGLISH
Antworten	To answer
Arbeiten	To work
Blicken	To look, to glance
Brauchen	To need
Danken	To thank
Fragen	To ask
Gehen	To go
Glauben	To believe
Heißen	To be named, to be called
Kommen	To come
Kosten	To cost
Kaufen	To buy
Lernen	To learn
Lieben	To love
Machen	To do
Mieten	To rent
Rauchen	To smoke
Reisen	To travel
Reservieren	To reserve
Sagen	To say
Schicken	To send sth.
Sehen	To see
Spielen	To play
Suchen	To search for sth
Tanzen	To dance

Telefonieren	To phone sm
Tun	To do smh
Wandern	To hike
Warten	To wait
Wohnen	To live
Zeigen	To show, to indicate

In addition to this, the conjugation of powerful verbs generally follows a regular pattern.

On the other hand, the vowels that are found in their stems go through some minor spelling adjustments. The table that follows provides a listing of some of the most frequently used strong verbs in the German language:

GERMAN	ENGLISH
Backen	To bake
Bleiben	To remain
Beginnen	To begin sth
Fahren	To drive
Fallen	To fall
Essen	To eat
Fliegen	To fly
Geben	To give
Halten	To stop
Helfen	To help
Laufen	To run
Leiden	To suffer
Lesen	To read

Nehmen	To take sth
Schlafen	To sleep
Sprechen	To speak
Treffen	To meet
Trinken	To drink

Strong Verbs that have a lot of power tend to have conjugated forms that are irregular, which means they do not follow the regular pattern.

Unfortunately, German has a number of significant and often used verbs that are irregular.

Inseparable prefixes

An inseparable prefix verb is a type of verb in which the beginning syllable of the verb is never separated from the root of the verb in any tense or conjugated form of the verb. It is always the case that these syllables are unstressed, which means that this part of the word does not get additional emphasis when it is spoken.

They are nearly always composed of relatively small groupings of letters that together form a particular meaning. Take, for instance, the English prefixes 'pre-' (meaning 'before') and 'dis-' (meaning 'not' or 'none')

In German, prefixes that are always inseparable are **-be, -emp, -ent, -er, -ge, -miss, -ver, -zer. *Zum Beispiel:***

- bezaubern (to enchant)
- empfehlen (to recommend)
- entfliehen (to flee from)
- erneuern (to renew)
- gefallen (to be pleasing)
- missfallen(to displease)

- verhungern (to starve)
- zerstören (to destroy)

REFLEXIVE VERBS

A verb is said to be reflexive if the direct object of the verb is the same thing as the subject of the verb. Or, to put it in an easier way for you, it is when the person doing the action to themselves is the one doing the deed, **zum Beispiel:** *'ich wasche mich'. (I wash myself)*

How do you know when the verb is reflexive? Easy! You can spot a reflexive German verb by its use of **'sich'** (self) in the infinitive form. Some examples of it are:

- ***sich ärgern*** - to get angry
- ***sich freuen*** - to be happy
- ***sich hinlegen*** - to lie down

These verbs undergo conjugation by switching the *'sich'* to reflect the subject or object of the action. After that, add the necessary ends to the verbs.

Verbs that are considered irregular do not totally adhere to the usual pattern of conjugation. The verb 'to have' (**haben**) and 'to be' (**sein**) are two of the most common and famous examples of irregular verbs.

You should keep in mind that some German verbs are considered to be mixed verbs because, depending on the tense, they can either have a weak or strong tendency. Only in the present tense do they behave like weak verbs, though.

However, similar to powerful verbs, the spelling of their stems shifts slightly when they are conjugated in the past tense, and there are no consistent patterns to follow. Verbs that fall under this category in German include the following:

- *brennen* – to burn
- *bringen* – to bring

- *denken* – to think
- *kennen* – to know a person or a place
- *nennen* – to name
- *rennen* – to run
- *senden* – to send
- *wenden* - to turn/ wind
- *wissen* - to know a fact

Aktivität

1. Write down the meanings of the given verbs and also make sentences using the same:

- Denken _____
- Schlafen _____
- Tragen _____
- Treffen _____
- Denken _____
- Gehen _____
- Bleiben _____
- Backen _____
- Warten _____
- Tun _____
- Rauchen _____
- Sagen _____
- Schicken _____
- Tanzen _____
- Lieben _____
- Glauben _____
- Geben _____
- Fliegen _____
- Lesen _____

We hope you are not too tired, we have so much more to do! E*s macht Spaß, oder?*

With our **'learn German in 30 days bundle'** you will definitely enjoy these topics!

In addition to everything so far, you are aware that German verbs are conjugated in order to reflect the time of the action as well as the person who carried it out.

You are now ready to start studying some regular German verbs that are also quite useful.

In addition to this, you will become familiar with the various forms of the verbs ***sein und haben***, which are widely considered to be the most important verbs in the German language.

Now, let's also quickly go over the conjugations of some of the most important verbs in German:

SEIN

- ich ***bin*** - I am
- du ***bist*** - you (singular, informal) are
- er/sie/es/man ***ist*** - he/she/it/ one is
- wir ***sind*** - we are
- ihr ***seid*** - you (plural, informal) are
- Sie ***sind*** - they/you (formal) are

HABEN

- Ich ***habe***
- du ***hast***
- er/sie/es/man ***hat***
- wir ***haben***
- ihr ***habt***
- Sie ***haben***

The initial words that have not been highlighted are, in essence, the pronouns that are written in German. The conjugated versions of the verbs in the present tense are emphasized in the second set of words, which also match the appropriate pronouns.

For instance, the first line has the words ich, which imply 'I', and bin, which means 'am'.

This conjugation can be seen in action in the following example sentence:

- *Ich **bin** größer als mein Vater* (I am taller than my father)

Sein is a powerful verb, or, to put it another way, it is one of the many German irregular verbs that you will need to be familiar with. This indicates that the pattern of conjugation for normal verbs is not followed by this verb form in any way.

It is important to keep in mind that verbs that accept **sein** in the present tense will also accept it as the auxiliary in the past perfect tense of the verb. Zum Beispiel:

- *Ich **war** gereist* (I had traveled)

MODAL VERBS

A modal verb is a sort of verb that, depending on the context in which it is used, may signify probability, capability, permission, request, capacity, suggestion, order, obligation, advice, or recommendation.

It's possible that all of this information is a lot to take in. Fortunately, there are only six of these words to master when speaking German.

The following are six modal verbs in the German language:

- **können** - can
- **dürfen** - may
- **mögen** - like
- **müssen** - must
- **sollen** - should
- **wollen** - want

Their conjugations will also clear your doubts about all the conjugations in german language, to know more about their conjugations, look at the given table:

PRESENT

	müssen	können	dürfen	sollen	wollen	mögen	möchten

ich	muss	kann	darf	soll	will	mag	möchte
du	musst	kannst	darfst	sollst	willst	magst	möchtest
er/ sie/ es	muss	kann	darf	soll	will	mag	möchte
wir	müssen	können	dürfen	sollen	wollen	mögen	möchten
ihr	müsst	könnt	dürft	sollt	wollt	mögt	möchtet
sie/ Sie	müssen	können	dürfen	sollen	wollen	mögen	möchten

SIMPLE PAST

	müssen	**können**	**dürfen**	**sollen**	**wollen**	**mögen**	**möchten**
ich	musste	konnte	durfte	sollte	wollte	mochte	wollte
du	musstest	konntest	durftest	solltest	wolltest	mochtest	wolltest
er/ sie/ es	musste	konnte	durfte	sollte	wollte	mochte	wollte
wir	mussten	konnten	durften	sollten	wollten	mochten	wollten
ihr	musstet	konntet	durftet	solltet	wolltet	mochtet	wolltet
sie/ Sie	mussten	konnten	durften	sollten	wollten	mochten	wollten

ACHTUNG!!

möchten is in fact the subjunctive form of mögen, but nowadays it is used in the present tense as a separate modal verb (for past tenses, we use wollen).

Aktivität

1. **Use the correct form of action verbs in Present tense in the given sentences:**

- Blake (reservieren) _____ ein Hotelzimmer.

- Blake und Chloe (warten) _____ auf den Bus.

- Wir (fragen) _____ nach der Adresse.

- Er (brauchen) _____ ein Taxi.

- Ich (lernen) _____ Deutsch.

- Chloe (essen) _____ Bratwurst.

- Chloe (treffen) _____ ihre deutsche Freundin.

- Du (sprechen) _____ sehr gut Englisch.

- Karl (fahren)_____ nach Köln.

- Der Bus (halten)_____ vor der Kirche.

2. Use the correct form of verb in present perfect tense:

- (laufen) Wir _____ den ganzen Tag _____

- (kaufen) Sie hat gestern ein neues Kleid _____

- (kochen) Blake _____ heute Morgen Pasta _____

- (lieben) Ich _____ diese Schuhe _____

- (reisen) Wir _____ letzten Monat durch Europa _____

- (machen) Du _____ einen Fehler _____

- (treffen) Blake und Chloe _____ sich vor drei Jahren _____

- (bleiben) Wir _____ zu Hause _____

- (anrufen) Ich _____ dein Büro _____

- (send) Blake _____ Chloe ein Jahr lang jeden Tag Blumen _____

3. Use the correct form of the verb in simple past tense form:

- Ich (haben) _____ meine Haustierkatze.

- Deine Eltern (arbeiten) _____ hart.

- Der Regen (beginnen) _____ zu fallen.

- Es (sein) _____ eine gute Erfahrung.

- Wir (wohnen) _____ in den Bergen.

4. Use the correct form of werden and verb using the future tense in given sentences:

- (essen) Ich _____ später _____

- (sehen) Sie _____ einen Film _____

- (gewinnen) Du _____ _____

- (sein) Sie _____ in ein paar Minuten hier _____

- (heiraten) Chloe _____ Blake im Herbst _____

KEY TAKEAWAYS!

Some important points which we covered in this chapter are:
- *The six types of tenses in the German language with their explanations and examples*
- *The types of verbs along with their meanings and explanations*
- *The moods in the German language*
- *Weak, strong, regular and irregular verbs*
- *Conjugations in the German language and how to read and understand the conjugations*
- *How to conjugate as per different tenses*
- *What are modal verbs and how to conjugate them correctly*
- *We also introduced new LESEN exercises to increase our German fluency and knowledge of the sentence structure*
- *New vocabulary, many German verb tables and their meanings*

ANTWORTEN! ANSWER KEY

Page 17, Q1
Present
- reserviert
- Warten
- Fragen
- Braucht
- Lerne
- Isst
- Trifft
- Spricht
- Fährt

-   hält

Page 18, Q2

Present Perfect

-   sind, gelaufen
-   hat, gekauft
-   hat, gekocht
-   habe, geliebt
-   sind, gereist
-   hast, gemacht
-   haben, getroffen
-   sind, geblieben
-   habe, angerufen
-   hat, gesandt

Page 19, Q3

Simple Past

-   Hatte
-   Arbeiteten
-   Began
-   war
-   wohnten

Page 19, Q4

Future

-   werde, essen
-   werden, sehen
-   wirst, gewinnen
-   werden, sein
-   wird, heiraten

SCHLUSSFOLGERUNG/ CONCLUSION

Ach, endlich!!

How did it go? The German tenses, verbs, and modal verbs, as well as everything else we've covered, should now be at your fingertips, we hope you were also as consistent as we were. *Jetzt sind wir fertig*, we have almost completely covered the basics of German. *Es war kinderleicht? Ja?* We told you!!

Gratulieren on completing your 30 days challenge with us!! We are confident that you have enjoyed studying German with us so far thanks to our and our **'Learn German in 30 days bundle!'**

We tried to keep the book simple, with easily explained concepts, activities that are concise and simple to grasp, content that is relevant and up to date, sections that provide a quick glimpse of the important information (*Takeaways*), activities that are both enjoyable and educational, and many chapters beginning at the A1 level with easy to understand concepts and rules, this course was specially crafted to make you confident in your language skills and we hope we were successful!

Now, then, what do we say when we have to say goodbye in German? *Was*? *Auf Wiedersehen? Ja!* *Sehr gut!!*
Have a successful and fun language journey, *tschüß*!

Bis bald! Alles Gute!

BOOK 2

German Phrasebook for Adult Beginners: Over 2500 Essential Words And Phrases You Must Know!

Common German Words & Phrases For Everyday Conversation and Travel

INTRODUCTION

Mancher hat das Herz auf der Zunge

'Hallo zusammen! Wie geht es Ihnen?'

These are the questions which are usually asked when you meet new people, for example on a vacation or a work conference. Learning German opens up a world of possibilities; not only do you gain insight into a new **'Kultur'** and way of life, but you also become fluent in it's lingo.

Germany has been a tourist hotspot for quite some time, and with expanding opportunities, it has also become a popular destination for those looking to relax and unwind on vacation.

This book is a useful guide for anyone hoping to practice their German, with basic phrases which are easy to grasp and would help you sound like a native, and more so, there are no cons to learning German! With that, **'sollten wir anfangen?'**

The fundamentals of the German conversations are presented in this **'German Phrasebook for Adult Beginners'.** We will cover all the basic important scenarios that would help you to hold a conversation with the natives like a pro, we hope you will like it!

Now, **'Kennen wir uns schon?'** If not, we would like to take this opportunity to say **'Hallo'**. See how easy that was to understand even if German is new to you, we will make sure that by the time we get done with this book, you will not only know and understand this line but also all the basic German greetings! Excited?

In our book **'German Phrasebook for Adult Beginners'**, we will find out what exactly does each typical day in the lives of Germans involve? It includes things like dialogues, conversations, and expressions, as well as any and all other forms of communication that we engage in so that we can be understood.

In each nation and culture, people have developed distinctive ways of communicating with one another, including hand gestures, pronouns, phrases, idioms, and other forms of language. In this book, you will study some of those for German, so let's get started without wasting any more *'Zeit'*!

Los geht's!!

KAPITEL 1

'Das Ziel der Wünsche steht niemals still.'
von George Gerhard Reisenberg

Wie heißen Sie? What is your name?

'What is your name?' is one of the most commonly and frequently asked questions, it doesn't matter what country you live in or which language you speak, this question is asked everywhere. So let's start our journey with this only!

You need to use a particular short phrase, *'**Wie heißen Sie?**' (VEE HYE-sen ZEE)*, to question someone about their name. Actually, the phrase doesn't contain the word 'name' at all. The phrase's meaning is more akin to 'What are you called?'
This is the sentence you say when you meet someone new and want to get their name.

The reply is straightforward: 'My name is_____ ,' or 'Ich heiße___' You simply insert the proper name where the blank is missing. Just like we frequently do in English, it's customary to provide the initial name while responding with a last name. Consider these instances, **zum Beispiel**:

- *Wie heißen Sie? Ich heiße Karl.*
- *Wie heißen Sie? Ich heiße Maria.*
- *Wie heißen Sie? Ich heiße Braun, Herbert Braun.*
- *Wie heißen Sie? Ich heiße Schmidt, Peter Schmidt.*

If you're unsure but think you know someone's name, you can ask: 'Heißen Sie Sabine?' by putting the verb *'**heißen**'* in front of the subject *'**Sie**.'*
The response could be either positive (ja) or negative (nein) zum beispiel:

- ***Heißen Sie George?*** *Is your name George?.*

- *Ja, ich heiße George.* Yes, of course, George is my name.
- *Heißen Sie Schröder?* Is your name Schröder?
- *Nein, ich heiße Schäfer, Angelika Schäfer.* No, my name is Schäfer, Angelika Schäfer.

Aktivität:

Ask what someone's name is using the first word in each pair. Respond with the name that is second in the pair. For example, if the first words in the pair are 'der Mann', ask yourself, Wie heißt der Mann? (What's the man's name?) Then use the second name in the pair to respond: Der Mann heißt Beau. (The man's name is Beau.)

- die Frau/ Maria Charlotte
- _____
- der Student (the male student)/Hans
- _____
- die Studentin (the female student)/Christine
- _____
- der Ausländer (foreigner)/Jojo Hans
- _____

How are you? Wie geht es Ihnen?

This is a common greeting which is also asked across every language. Depending on who you are speaking to, 'How are you?' might be asked in either a formal or informal manner.

The personal pronouns *ich*, *du*, and *Sie* must also be used in the dative case. The formal version of 'How are you?' is

- *Wie geht es Ihnen? (How are you? Literally, 'How is it going?')*

More informally, you use *dir*:

- *Wie geht es dir?*

If you really know someone well, you can go for the most casual version of the question:

- *Wie geht's? (How's it going?)*

The query *'Wie geht es Ihnen?'* is frequently just a way to say hello in English, and nobody expects you to respond. Yet, in German, people typically predict your response. How are you is a question that can be answered in the ways listed below:

- *Danke, gut. / Gut, danke.* (Thanks, I'm fine. / Fine, thanks.) The literal translation would be 'Thanks, good.' / 'Good, thanks.'
- *Sehr gut.* (Very good.)
- *Ganz gut.* (Pretty good.)
- *Es geht so, so.* The German expression actually means 'it goes okay okay' and implies that it's not going too well.
- *Nicht so gut.* (Not so good.)

In the same way that it is in English, the reply is typically followed by the question 'And (how are) you?' which is a straightforward inquiry. the official version first:

- *Und Ihnen?* (And you? formal)
- *Und dir?* (And you? informal)

Telling your name, the German way!

Introductions are frequently needed for meeting and greeting. You can use one of the two methods listed below to introduce yourself to people. Among them is:

- Mein Name ist _____ (My name is _____)

There also is a verb that expresses the same idea, heißen, which means 'to be called':

- Ich heiße _____ (My name is _____)

To introduce someone else, all you need are these phrases:

- Das ist _____ (This is _____)

Then you simply add the name of the person. To indicate that you're introducing a friend, you say:

- Das ist meine Freundin (f) / mein Freund (m) _____ (This is my friend_____)

If you're introduced to somebody in a slightly more formal setting, you can express 'Nice to meet you' by saying:

- Freut mich. (I'm pleased.)

The person you have been introduced to might then reply:

- Mich auch. (Me too.)

In the following interactions, each participant introduces themselves to the other. One example of a young person who meets someone in a relaxed setting, like a party, is as follows:

- *George: Hallo, wie heißt Du? (Hello, what's your name?)*
- *Anja: Ich heiße Anja. Und Du? (My name is Anja. And you?)*
- *George: George. Und wer ist das? (George. And who is that?)*
- *Anja: Das ist meine Freundin Anne. (This is my friend Anne.)*

An exchange between two men is shown here, with one introducing his wife:

- *Herr Stohl: Guten Abend, Herr Friedrich! (Good evening, Mr. Friedrich!)*
- *Herr Friedrich: Guten Abend, Herr Stohl. Darf ich Ihnen meine Frau vorstellen? (Good evening! Mr. Stohl. May I introduce you to my wife?)*
- *Herr Stohl: Guten Abend, Frau Friedrich! Freut mich sehr, Sie kennenzulernen. (Good evening, Mrs. Friedrich! Very nice to meet you.)*
- *Frau Friedrich: Ganz meinerseits, Herr Stohl. (Likewise, Mr. Stohl.)*

Woher kommen Sie? Where are you from?

You learn how to identify your hometown or country in this part, as well as how to ask others where they are from and what languages they speak. To accomplish all of these things, you must become proficient with the verb **sein** (to be). This verb is used in the sentences 'this is' and 'I am'. It's irregular, though, so you'll just have to commit it to memory, but you know we will help you achieve that with our '**German Phrasebook for Adult Beginners**'

- *ich bin*
- *du bist (informal)*

- *Sie sind (formal)*
- *er, sie, es ist*
- *wir sind*
- *ihr seid (informal)*
- *Sie sind (formal)*
- *sie sind*

You simply need to choose whether to address someone informally with *du, ihr*, or formally with *Sie* to question where they're from. Next, you pick one of these three options to answer the question 'Where are you from?'

- Wo kommen Sie her?
- Wo kommst du her?
- Wo kommt ihr her?

To say where you're from in German, the magic words are:

- Ich komme aus _____ (I come from _____)
- Ich bin aus _____ (I am from _____)

These few words are capable of conveying a great deal of meaning. They are employed by nations, governments, and urban areas. ***Zum Beispiel:***

- Ich komme aus Amerika. (I come from America.)
- Ich bin aus Pennsylvania. (I am from Pennsylvania.)
- Ich komme aus Zürich. (I come from Zurich.)
- Ich komme aus Wien. (I am from Vienna.)
- Meine Freundin kommt aus Lyon. (My friend comes from Lyon.)
- Wir sind aus Frankreich. (We are from France.)

ACHTUNG!!

The feminine definite article, die, is used with the names of some nations and places. One such nation is the United States. In German, you say 'Ich bin aus den USA' (I'm *from the USA) Or, you may try the tongue-twister 'Ich bin aus den Vereinigten Staaten'. (I'm from the United States).*

Learning About Other Countries

Whereas the English language typically uses the adjective form of a country's name to denote nationality (z.B., 'She is american'), Germans prefer to use a noun. Furthermore, these nouns for different nations also have genders, as you likely already know from studying German. Hence, a male American is called an **Amerikaner** and a female American is called an **Amerikanerin**.

'Countries' in German is '*Länder*' and the singular is '*das Land*'. This is connected to the English word 'land', whose original meaning centered more on the physical landscape of the land itself than on the governmental boundaries that surrounded it.

In our book '**German Phrasebook for Adult Beginners**' we have provided you with a list of the majority of countries, broken down by continent. Because they are all, thankfully, rather close to the names in English, it shouldn't be too difficult to commit them to memory.

African countries in German

A population census revealed that minorities holding passports from African countries make up one percent of Germany's total population. The majority of these minorities hail from Morocco, Eritrea, and Nigeria. There are also a great number of people who, on paper, hold German citizenship but whose roots lie in at least one of the following African nations:

ENGLISCH	DEUTSCH
Algeria	Algerien
Angola	Angola
Cameroon	Kamerun
Cape Verde	Kap Verde
Egypt	Ägypten

Republic of the Congo	Die Republik Kongo
The Democratic Republic of the Congo	Die Demokratische Republik Kongo
Equatorial Guinea	Äquatorialguinea
Ghana	Ghana
Ethiopia	Äthiopien
Ivory Coast	Die Elfenbeinküste
Kenya	Kenia
Libya	Libyen
Mauritius	Mauritius
Morocco	Marokko
Mozambique	Mosambik
Nigeria	Nigeria
Rwanda	Ruanda
Senegal	Senegal
Somalia	Somalia
South Africa	Südafrika
Sudan	Sudan
Syria	Syrien
Tunisia	Tunesien
Uganda	Uganda
Zimbabwe	Simbabwe

American countries in German

Here is a list of all the American nations in German, starting with Canada and going all the way down to Chile. Let's have a look, *los geht's!*

ENGLISCH	DEUTSCH
Argentina	Argentinien
Belize	Belize
Bolivia	Bolivien
Brazil	Brasilien
Canada	Kanada
Chile	Chile
Colombia	Kolumbien
Costa Rica	Costa Rica
Ecuador	Ecuador
Nicaragua	Nicaragua
Puerto Rico	Puerto Rico
Dominican Republic	Die Dominikanische Republik
Jamaica	Jamaika
Mexico	Mexiko
Panama	Panama
Paraguay	Paraguay
Peru	Peru
Venezuela	Venezuela
Trinidad and Tobago	Trinidad und Tobago
United States	Vereinigte Staaten

Countries of Asia in German

In Germany, you'll come across a lot of people having Asian ancestry. With nearly 4% of the German population, Turks make up the largest minority group. In fact, more than 200,000 people live in Berlin alone who identify as Turkish. Have a look at the table to know German names of Asian countries:

ENGLISCH	DEUTSCH
Armenia	Armenien
Azerbaijan	Aserbaidschan
Bangladesh	Bangladesch
Cambodia	Kambodscha
China	China
India	Indien
Indonesia	Indonesien
Iran	Iran
Iraq	Irak
Japan	Japan
Jordan	Jordanien
Kazakhstan	Kasachstan
North Korea	Nordkorea
South Korea	Südkorea
Mongolia	Die Mongolei
Malaysia	Malaysia
Lebanon	Der Libanon
Myanmar	Myanmar
Oman	Der Oman
Pakistan	Pakistan
Palestine	Palästina
Philippines	Die Philippinen
Qatar	Katar
Saudi Arabia	Saudi-Arabien
Singapore	Singapur

Sri Lanka	Sri Lanka
Thailand	Thailand
Turkey	Die Türkei
United Arab Emirates	Vereinigte Arabische Emirate
Uzbekistan	Usbekistan
Vietnam	Vietnam
Yemen	Der Jemen

European countries in German

Did you know that the term Europe comes from the Phoenician princess Europa, who was a mythological figure in Greek culture? Europe is the name of the continent. As a result, 'Europa' is the name for Europe in German, Spanish, Italian, and other languages.

ENGLISCH	DEUTSCH
Andorra	Andorra
Albania	Albanien
Austria	Österreich
Belgium	Belgien
Bulgaria	Bulgarien
Croatia	Kroatien
Cyprus	Zypern
Czechia	Tschechien
Denmark	Dänemark
Finland	Finnland
France	Frankreich
Germany	Deutschland

Greece	Griechenland
Hungary	Ungarn
Iceland	Island
Ireland	Irland
Italy	Italien
Lithuania	Litauen
Luxembourg	Luxemburg
The Netherlands	Die Niederlande
Norway	Norwegen
Poland	Polen
Portugal	Portugal
Romania	Rumänien
Russia	Russland
Serbia	Serbien
Slovakia	Die Slowakei
Slovenia	Slowenien
Spain	Spanien
Sweden	Schweden
Switzerland	Die Schweiz
Ukraine	Die Ukraine
United Kingdom	Vereinigtes Königreich

Oceanian countries in German

You would be floating in the water of the East coast of New Zealand if you dug a hole from Germany to the opposite side of the planet. Nothing is farther away than the nations and islands of Oceania, but fortunately for those of us wanting to escape the chilly weather in Germany, Samoa is only a few flights away.

ENGLISCH	DEUTSCH
Australia	Australien
Federated States of Micronesia	Föderierte Staaten von Mikronesien
Fiji	Fidschi
Kiribati	Kiribati
Papua New Guinea	Papua-Neuguinea
Samoa	Samoa
Solomon Islands	Die Salomoninseln
Tonga	Tonga
Vanuatu	Vanuatu
New Zealand	Neuseeland

Which Languages Can You Speak?

The verb *Sprechen* (to speak) and the name of the language are combined to let people know what language you speak. But be careful: Despite the fact that the adjective and the language for a nation or country are the same, you uppercase the adjective when it is used to describe the language on its own:

- *Ich spreche Deutsch.* (I speak german.)
- *Sprichst du Englisch?* is the phrase to use when asking someone if they speak English.
- *Sprechen Sie Englisch?* Do you speak English? (formal)

LESEN MACHT SPAß!!

Eine typische Studentenwoche

Montags habe ich frei. Es finden keine Vorlesungen statt. Am Morgen wiederhole ich, was ich gelernt habe. Mittags treffe ich mich mit Freunden, die auch frei haben. Bei gutem Wetter sitzen wir im Park, bei schlechtem Wetter treffen wir uns in meiner Wohnung. Wir spielen Brettspiele und reden über unsere Woche. Nicht alle meine Freunde studieren dasselbe wie ich. Dienstag bis Donnerstag muss ich an die Universität. Ich habe von acht (8) Uhr morgens bis siebzehn (17) Uhr abends Unterricht. Ich studiere das Fach Geschichte. Freitags haben wir praktischen Unterricht in einem Museum. Ich kann meine Fähigkeiten aus dem Unterricht im Museum gut anwenden und ich mache wertvolle Erfahrungen. Samstags schreibe ich an meinen Hausaufgaben. Es ist mühsam, aber ich mache gute Fortschritte. In der Regel verbringe ich samstags sechs (6) bis acht (8) Stunden mit dem Schreiben. Am Sonntag habe ich frei. Ich lese Dinge, die mich interessieren und treibe Sport. Meine Freunde und ich spielen sonntags oft Fußball. Das war meine Woche. Wie sieht eure Woche aus?

A typical week in the life of students

'I have Mondays off. There are no lectures. In the morning I repeat what I have learned. At noon, I meet with friends who also have the day off. In good weather we sit in the park, in bad weather we meet in my apartment. We play board games and talk about our week. Not all my friends study the same as me. Tuesday through Thursday I have to go to the university. I have classes from eight (8) in the morning until five (5) at night. I study the subject of history. On Fridays we have practical classes in a museum. I can use my skills from class well in the museum and I gain valuable experience. On Saturdays I complete my homework. It is tedious, but I make good progress. I usually spend six (6) to eight (8) hours writing on Saturdays. On Sunday, I have a day off. I read things that interest me and exercise. My friends and I often play soccer on Sundays. That was my week. What does your week look like?'

FRAGEN!

- Was machst du am Montag?
- Studieren alle deine Freunde dasselbe wie du? Wann beginnt der Unterricht und wann endet er? Was machst du freitags?
- Was machst du am Sonntag?
- Was machst du Montags bei schlechtem Wetter?

WORTSCHATZ!

- frei haben – to not have to work
- typisch – typical
- die Vorlesung – the lecture
- stattfinden – to take place wiederholen – to repeat
- sich treffen – to meet up

- spielen – to play
- reden – to talk
- alle – all
- studieren – to study
- dasselbe – the same
- das Fach – the subject
- praktisch – practical
- der Unterricht – the lesson
- die Fähigkeit – the ability
- anwenden – to put to use
- wertvoll – valuable
- die Erfahrung – the experience
- die Hausaufgabe – the homework
- mühsam – troublesome
- der Fortschritt – the progress
- in der Regel – usually
- den Samstag verbringen – to spend the Saturday
- Dinge die mich interessieren – things that interest me
- Sport treiben – to do sports
- Fußball – soccer
- aussehen wie – to look like

KEY TAKEAWAYS!

In this chapter, we learned these things:
- How to have basic conversations about the most important topics in German
- How to discuss your country in German (with examples)
- The names of several countries in both the English and German languages
- The foundations of having simple discussions in German
- LESEN MACHT SPAß: Reading is enjoyable, and doing so will assist you in expanding your German vocabulary and enhancing your reading abilities.
- The Wortschatz part that comes after the reading passages will help you expand your vocabulary!

ANSWERS/ ANTWORTEN

PG 137, Q1

- Wie heißt die Frau?

- Wie heißt der Student?

- Wie heißt die Studentin?

- Wie heißt der Ausländer?

Well, this was all about the countries in German language and also how to use them in basic conversations, now we hope you enjoyed this too, because we sure did!

Es war spaßig! Now shall we move forward to the next chapter in our book '**German Phrasebook for Adult Beginners**' and learn how to introduce us to the German way?

Sind Sie aufgeregt? Because we are, see you in **Kapitel 2!**

Bis bald!

KAPITEL 2

'Nicht die Übung macht den Meister, sondern der Ernstfall'

von Billy

'Hallo zusammen! Wie geht es Ihnen?'

Wie geht es Ihnen? We are sure you know this statement and the answer to this statement by now! ***Oder?***

The fundamentals of the German language were presented in our book 1 **'Learn German for beginners'** and if you've been following along with us for the past month, you should already be very well versed in the language. Now we are here in **Kapitel 2**, and we will learn how to introduce ourselves!

We would like to take this opportunity to say ***'Hallo'*** once more. So, we are sure that many of you who are learning German are eager to get started on our next adventure, which will cover the German words and phrases that are used most frequently in this book **'German Phrasebook for Adult Beginners'**, we will find out what exactly does each typical day in the lives of Germans involve?

One of the first things you'll usually learn when you begin studying German fluently is how to introduce yourself. There are a number of reasons why this specific topic is important.

To begin with, you will introduce yourself in German to everyone you encounter in a German-speaking country. Since you'll use the same words so frequently when speaking German, it makes sense to memorize them by memory when you first start studying the language.

Second, even if you are a complete newbie, learning the self-introduction words is not too difficult. Being able to express yourself in a foreign language so rapidly boosts your confidence and inspires you to learn more.

Therefore don't think twice and start learning German for introductions with the help of our **'German Phrasebook for Adult Beginners'** and ***Los geht's!***

We have already covered the basics like 'how are you?' and 'what country do you come from?' and 'what languages do you speak?' in German but there is so much more to you than that, your introduction involves family, your pet, and everything related to you, so let's dive in!

Place of residence

- Ich wohne in _____ . I live in (city/country).

Zum Beispiel:

Ich wohne in Berlin. (I live in Berlin)

Ich wohne in Australien. (I live in Australia)

Ich wohne in der Schweiz. (I live in Switzerland)

ACHTUNG!!
Here the preposition in also takes the Dative case, so you have to conjugate the article in dative if the country is used with the article.

Ich bin ledig. (I am single.)

This short phrase can be used to let the attractive person at the party know that you are single, as well as when a German document (and there is no shortage of paperwork in Germany) asks you about your marital status.

And if you want to tell people that you are married, you can simply state ***'Ich bin verheiratet'*** (I am married) z.B.:

- *Sonja ist ledig.*

- *Johannes ist verheiratet.*

Meine Handynummer ist... (My phone number is...)

You would have guessed from this statement that a mobile phone in Germany is referred to as a Handy, probably because you can carry it around in your hand. z.B:
- Meine Handynummer ist 948263.
- Die Handynummer von Anja ist 93744.

Ich studiere... (I am studying...)

Whether your job is as an architect, a doctor, a taxi driver, or if you're still a student, there are many occupational words to learn in German.

You can begin with the simple question, *'Was sind Sie von Beruf?'* This means, *'What's your occupation?'* There are so many different types of occupations, and we can be anything we set our mind to, *oder*? Let's have a look at some of the most commonly used occupations and their German names!

Before we proceed, just remember that German speakers typically omit the 'a' or 'an' when stating things like 'I'm a student' or 'He's an architect'. Instead, you'll say *'Er ist Architekt'* or *'Ich bin Student(in)'* (no 'ein' or 'eine').

You should only use *'ein'* or *'eine'* if an adjective is included. For instance, *'sie ist eine neue Architektin'* (she is a new architect) and *'er ist ein guter Student'* (he is a good student).

Berufe (Professions)

The most common occupations and their German names are listed in the table given below. Remember that in German, every occupation has both a feminine and a masculine form.

Only in instances where there is a difference in English or when there is more than just the cusTimmyary *-in ending* (such as in *der Arzt und die Ärztin*) have we listed the feminine form (as in waiter and waitress).

The feminine is used in situations where the German feminine form is more common as well as for occupations that are more likely to be held by women, such as that of a nurse or secretary.

ENGLISCH	DEUTSCH
architect	der Architekt
auto mechanic	der Automechaniker
baker	der Bäcker
bank teller	der Bankangestellte, die Bankangestellte
bricklayer/ stonemason	der Maurer
Broker	der Makler
stock broker	der Börsenmakler
real estate agent	der Immobilienmakler
bus driver	der Busfahrer
computer programer	der Programmierer, die Programmiererin
cook	Chef, der Koch, der Chefkoch die Köchin, die Chefköchin
doctor, physician	der Arzt, die Ärztin
employee, white-collar worker	der Angestellte, die Angestellte
employee, blue-collar worker	der Arbeiter, die Arbeiterin
IT worker	Angestellte/Angestellter in der Informatik
cabinetmaker	der Tischler
journalist	der Journalist
secretary	der Sekretär, die Sekretärin
musician	der Musiker
Student	der Schüler, die Schülerin
photographer	der Fotograf, die Fotografin
student (college, univ.)*	der Student, die Studentin

taxi driver	der Taxifahrer
teacher	der Lehrer, die Lehrerin
waiter - waitress	der Kellner/die Kellnerin
worker, laborer	der Arbeiter
truck/lorry driver	der Lkw-Fahrer/der Brummi Fahrer
nurse	der Krankenpfleger, die Krankenschwester

Ich bin _____ von Beruf. (literally means I'm _____ by profession.)

oder

Ich bin _____ . (I'm (profession)).

Zum Beispiel:

- *Ich bin Student/Studentin. (I am a student.)*
- *Ich bin Rentner/Rentnerin. (I am retired.)*
- *Ich bin Lehrer/Lehrerin von Beruf. (I'm a teacher.)*
- *Ich bin Programmierer/Programmiererin. (I'm a programmer.)*
- *Ich bin Arzt/Ärztin. – I'm a doctor.*

Ich mag... (I like...)

What about a short, effective phrase that can be used repeatedly? You can tell about your likes with this basic German sentence, see examples below:

- *Ich mag Pizza (I like pizza)*
- *Ich mag das Wochenende (I like the weekend)*
- *Ich mag das Wetter (I like the weather.)*

Age, birthday

Ich bin _____ Jahre alt. (I am (age) years old.)

oder

Ich bin _____. (I am (age)).

Mein Geburtstag ist im _____. (My birthday is in (month)).

Zum Beispiel:

- *Ich bin 26 (sechsundzwanzig) Jahre alt. (I'm 26 years old.)*
- *Ich bin 55 (fünfundfünfzig). – (I am 55.)*
- *Mein Geburtstag ist im August. (My birthday is in August.)*

Sprachen/Languages

Meine Muttersprache ist _____. (My mother tongue is (language))

oder

Ich spreche _____. (I speak (language)).

Ich lerne _____. (I am learning (language))

Zum Beispiel:
- *Meine Muttersprache ist Arabisch. (My mother tongue is Arabic.)*
- *Ich spreche Englisch, Französisch und Arabisch. (I speak English, French and Arabic.)*
- *Ich lerne Chinesisch und Deutsch. (I am learning Chinese and German.)*

Talking about family in German

Ich bin _____. (I'm (marital status)).

Ich bin ledig/verheiratet. (I'm single/married.)

Ich habe _____. (I have (children/siblings))

Zum beispiel:

- *Ich habe ein Kind/zwei Kinder. – I have a child/two children.*
- *Ich habe keine Kinder. – I don't have children.*
- *Ich habe 3 (drei) Geschwister. – I have 3 siblings.*
- *Ich habe keine Geschwister. – I don't have siblings.*

Family members in German

The german vocabulary for family members is given in the list below, have a look:

- die Familie, -n – family
- die Ehe,-n – marriage
- der Ehemann, die Ehemänner – husband
- die Ehefrau, die Ehefrauen – wife
- die Eltern – parents
- die Großeltern – grandparents
- die Mutter, die Mütter – mother
- der Vater, die Väter – father
- die Großmutter/die Oma,-s – grandmother
- der Großvater/der Opa,-s – grandfather
- das Kind, -er – child
- der Sohn, die Söhne – son
- die Tochter, die Töchter – daughter
- der Zwilling, -e – twin(s)
- die Geschwister – siblings
- der Bruder, die Brüder – brother
- die Schwester, -n – sister
- die Enkelkinder – grandchildren
- der Enkel – grandson
- die Enkelin, -nen – granddaughter
- die Tante,-n – aunt
- der Onkel – uncle

- der Neffe, -n – nephew
- die Nichte, -n – niece
- der Cousin, -s – male cousin
- die Cousine, -n – female cousin
- der Verwandte, -n – male relative
- die Verwandte,-n – female relative

Hobbies in German

Mein Hobby ist _____. (My hobby is (hobby))

Meine Hobbys sind _____. (My hobbies are (hobbies)).

Zum Beispiel:
- *Mein Hobby ist Musik. (My hobby is music.)*
- *Meine Hobbys sind singen und tanzen. (My hobbies are singing and dancing.)*
- *Mein Hobby ist Einkaufen. (My hobby is shopping.)*

How to say 'I like.../I don't like...' in German.

To say 'I like doing something' we can use the following sentences:

Ich _____ gerne. (I like (doing some activity))

Ich _____ nicht gerne. (I don't like (doing some activity))

Zum Beispiel:
- *Ich reise gerne. (I like traveling.)*
- *Ich koche nicht gerne. (I don't like cooking.)*
- *Ich lese gerne Bücher. (I like reading books.)*

To say 'I like something' we can use the given sentences:

Ich mag _____. (I like (something))

Ich mag _____ nicht. (I don't like (something))

Zum Beispiel:
- *Ich mag Sushi. – I like sushi.*
- *Ich mag Pizza nicht. – I don't like pizza.*
- *Ich mag Kaffee, aber ich mag Tee nicht. – I like coffee but I don't like*

To talk about your favorite things in German we can say:

Mein Lieblings... ist _____. (My favorite (food/movie/sport) is (name))

Zum Beispiel:
- *Mein Lieblingsessen ist Pizza. (My favorite food is Pizza.)*
- *Mein Lieblingssport ist Fußball. (My favorite sport is football.)*

Aktivität:
Complete the following dialogue between Timmy and Christy using informal phrases!

Christy: Hallo, ich bin Christy! _____ heißt du? (Hello, I'm Christy! What's your name?)

Timmy: Hi Christy, ich _____ Timmy! (Hi Christy, my name is Timmy)

Christy: Schön, dich kennenzulernen! Wie alt _____? (Nice to meet you! How old are you?)

Timmy: Ich _____ 22 Jahre alt. Wie _____ bist du? (I'm 22 years old. How old are you?)

Christy: _____ bin 21 Jahre alt. (I am 21 years old)

Timmy: Woher kommst _____? (Where are you from?)

Christy: Ich _____ aus England, und du? (I'm from England, and you?)

Timmy: _____ bin _____ Deutschland. (I'm from Germany)

Christy: Und _____ lebst du? (And where do you live?)

Timmy: Ich _____ in Berlin. (I live in Berlin)

LESEN MACHT SPAß!!

Eine neue Stadt

Ich bin neu in Berlin. Heute miete ich eine Wohnung. Es ist ein schöner Tag, weil die Sonne scheint und die Vögel singen. Ich stehe vor meiner neuen Wohnung. Ein Mann kommt heraus. Er grüßt mich. Es ist mein Vermieter. Er will mir die Wohnung zeigen. Gemeinsam gehen wir in das alte Haus. Im Treppenhaus ist es stickig und es riecht komisch. Wir gehen die Treppe nach oben, dann stehen wir vor der Wohnung. Es ist eine große, alte Tür. Die Wohnung ist sauber und neu. Das überrascht mich. Sie gefällt mir sehr gut, aber sie ist teuer. Ich überlege, ob ich sie mieten will. Wir gehen in alle Zimmer. In den Zimmern sind Möbel. Ein Bett, eine Küche und Schränke. Es ist alles da. Ich kann deshalb viel Geld sparen. Ich bin glücklich. Ich will die Wohnung mieten. Es ist kein Problem. Ich kann den Vertrag direkt unterschreiben. Endlich habe ich eine neue Wohnung. Sie gefällt mir am besten. Ich rufe meine Freundin an und erzähle ihr, wie glücklich ich bin.

A new state

'I am new in Berlin. Today I am renting an apartment. It's a beautiful day because the sun is shining and the birds are singing. I stand in front of my new apartment. A man comes out. He greets me. It is my landlord. He wants to show me the apartment. Together we went into the old house. It is stuffy in the stairwell and it smells funny. We go up the stairs, then we stand in front of the apartment. It is a big, old door. The apartment is clean and new. That surprises me. I like it very much, but it is expensive. I'm thinking about renting it. We go into all the rooms. There is furniture in the rooms. A bed, a kitchen and cupboards. It's all there. I can save a lot of money because of that. I am happy. If I want to rent this apartment. It is not a problem. I can sign the contract directly. Finally, I have a new apartment. I like it the most. I am calling my girlfriend and telling her how happy I am.'

Fragen

- Warum ist heute ein schöner Tag?
- Wer ist der Mann, der aus dem Haus kommt? Wie riecht es im Treppenhaus? Warum bist du überrascht?
- Warum kannst du so viel Geld sparen?

WORTSCHATZ!

- neu sein in – to be new in

- mieten – to rent
- der Vogel – the bird
- die Wohnung – the apartment heraus kommen – to walk out grüßen – to greet
- der Vermieter – the landlord
- nach oben - upwards
- zeigen – to show
- gemeinsam – together
- alt – old
- stickig – stifling
- riechen – to smell
- komisch – strange
- sauber – clean
- überraschen – to surprise
- gefallen – to like
- teuer – expensive
- die Möbel – the furniture
- der Schrank – the closet
- deshalb – therefore
- das Geld – the money
- sparen – to save up
- der Vertrag – the contract
- endlich – finally

KEY TAKEAWAYS!

In this chapter, we learned these things:
- How to correctly present yourself to others in the German language
- How to discuss the interests you have outside of work
- How to inquire about someone's basic introduction as well as their preferences and dislikes
- What are some of the basic ways that humans can communicate with one another?
- There are a few distinct ways to refer to each member of the family when speaking German.
- The essentials of having simple discussions in German.

- LESEN MACHT SPAß: Reading is enjoyable, and doing so will assist you in expanding your German vocabulary and enhancing your reading abilities.
- The Wortschatz part that comes after the reading passages will help you expand your vocabulary!

ANSWERS/ ANTWORTEN

PG 155

- Wie
- Heiße
- Bist
- Bin, alt
- Ich
- Du
- Komme
- Ich, aus
- Wo
- Lebe

Well, this was all about the basic introduction in German language and also how to use them in basic conversations, now we hope you enjoyed this too, because we sure did!

Es war spaßig! Now shall we move forward to the next chapter in our book '**German Phrasebook for Adult Beginners**' and learn how to introduce us to the German way?

Sind Sie aufgeregt? Because we are, see you in **Kapitel 3**!

Bis bald!

KAPITEL 3

Mögen sie dort blühen, wo Gott sie hingepflanzt hat
von Franz von Sales

'Hallo zusammen! Wie geht es Ihnen?'

Wie geht es Ihnen? We are sure you know this statement and the answer to this statement by now! ***Oder?***

The fundamentals of the German language were presented in our book 1 **'Learn German for beginners'** and if you've been following along with us for the past month, you should already be very well versed in the language. Now we are here in **Kapitel 3**, and we will learn the basic things in the German language such as most used idioms, phrases and words, without which the German language would be incomplete! We will also see how to order food in a German restaurant.

We will talk about the basic vocabulary in German language that will help you in sounding like a Deutscher and also have a look at their vocabulary to enhance your German language skills.
We have been working so hard this past month, with our 30 days challenge, we are sure that with the help of our **'German Phrasebook for Adult Beginners'** you will also be fluent in German in no time!

Los geht's!

How to ask for directions in German

The mentioned conversation starters which we have discussed so far make for excellent, worthwhile discussions. Nonetheless, you also have the need to be able to use public transportation and ask for directions if you need to travel to a specific location or the point.

Imagine that you are starving but are unable to locate the nearest Cafe. *'**Ich habe Hunger**'* (I am hungry) and *'**Ich habe Durst**'* (I am thirsty) are pretty straightforward to learn, but it is more helpful to know the whole German language used to inquire about the nearest restaurant or grocery store. Instead of making a general remark, let us learn about how to inquire about the basic directions in German language with the help of our **'German Phrasebook for Adult Beginners'**.

- **Wo finde ich...**
- ... einen Geldautomaten?... ein Taxi?... eine Toilette?
- Where do I find......a cash machine?...a taxi? ...a toilet?

- **Wo ist...**
- ... der Bahnhof? ... die Touristeninformation?
- Where is......the train station?...the tourist information?

- **Wie komme ich......**
- zum Kino?...zum Einkaufszentrum?...zum nächstgelegenen Supermarkt?
- How do I get ......to the movie theater?...to the mall?...to the closest Supermarket?

- **Ich habe mich verlaufen** (I've lost my way (while walking))
- **Ich habe mich verfahren** (I've lost my way (while driving))

- **Wann fährt......**
- der nächste Bus?... die nächste U-Bahn?...die nächste S-Bahn?...der nächste Zug?
- When comes...... the next bus?... the next subway?...the next suburban train?...the next train?
- **Wie viel kostet...**
- ... eine Fahrkarte nach Berlin? ...eine Tageskarte?
- How much is......a ticket to Berlin?....a day pass?

- **Ich bin unterwegs** (I am on my way)
- **Ich bin gleich da** (I am almost there)

How to place a meal order in German

Biergärten, or literally 'beer-gardens' (or more generally, 'rustic backyard settings' as they are known in Germany), are places where beer is served. But Germany is much more than just beer! The dynamic German food scene, which includes restaurants and inventive fast food, is one that shouldn't be missed.

ACHTUNG!!

When being served, you may hear, 'Die servieren ein halbes Schwein auf Toast' which translates to, 'They serve half a pig on a slice of toast'. If so, get prepared to wrap up your meal feeling incredibly satiated.

All the German words and phrases you need to order and eat successfully are included below:

- *Ich hätte gerne...* (I would like to have...)
- *Haben Sie...?* (Do you have..?)
- *Die Speisekarte* (the menu)
- *Was können Sie empfehlen?* (What can you recommend?)
- *Das ist alles, danke.* (That's all, thank you)
- *Das Essen schmeckt lecker!* (The food tastes very good!)
- *Zum Wohl! or Prost!*   (Cheers!)
- *Die Rechnung, bitte.* (The bill, please)
- *Ich möchte bitte zahlen.* (I would like to pay)
- *Kann ich mit EC-Karte zahlen?* (Do you take debit cards?)
- *Kann ich mit Kreditkarte bezahlen?* (Do you take credit cards?)
- *Stimmt so!* (Keep the change!)

Regional and colloquial terms in German

Speaking German fluently is one thing, but what about sounding like a native speaker? Or at least making an impression on those you meet when you are on your holiday in Germany. Getting there can be eased by learning some basic German lingo. You can even use regional terms if you know where the speaker is from or if you're visiting a particular area.

Slang's greatest benefit is that it really increases linguistic accessibility. When used with adjectives, it adds emphasis and deviates from the language's custom of having a lengthy vocabulary. *'Supergut'* (above good) originates from *'gut'* (good).

The majority of Germany's regions, as well as certain other German-speaking nations, have their own dialects when it comes to regional phrases. The fundamentals will be understood by all German speakers, so don't worry!

Simply said, learning regional slang is a fun approach to expand your cultural horizons and establish more meaningful connections with the community.

Here are some examples of colloquialisms and regional idioms to use:
- *Weißt du was ich meine?* (You know what I mean? Got it?)
- *Unglaublich, geht ja gar nicht!* (Unbelievable, that can't be!)
- *Das ist gehupft, wie gesprungen.* (It's all the same. It doesn't make a big difference.)
- *German phrase in Austria: Ghupft wia ghatscht.*
- *Nur keine Eile.* (Don't stress or rush.)
- *German phrase in Austria: Nur ned hudln.*
- *Mahlzeit!* (Going to lunch!)
- If greeted with the word 'Mahlzeit' in the hallway of your office, the best way to reply is 'Mahlzeit!' It doesn't get more German than that.
- *Jetzt mach mal hin!* (Hurry up/Get stuff done/Make a decision!) (Used in the right context, it can mean all three!)
- German phrase in Switzerland: *Chasch nöd dä Foifer und s'Weggli ha!*

GERMAN IDIOMS AND ALLTÄGLICHE (EVERYDAY) PHRASES

Did you know that the German language, just like the English language, has slang and idiomatic expressions?

Consider a situation in which a person who is just beginning to learn English overhears the phrase *'Get a load of her!'*

What must be going through his or her mind? When native English speakers attempt to learn German, the same thing happens.

They come across a number of strange idioms, and when they check the words up in a dictionary, the expressions don't appear to make all that much sense.

Because they are idioms or are just plain slang, it is impossible to translate them directly into another language.

Let's have a look at some fascinating German phrases in our book **'German Phrasebook for Adult Beginners'** and the idiomatic expressions that correspond to them in English:

- ***Der Apfel fällt nicht weit vom Stamm.*** *(The apple doesn't fall far from the stem.)*
- Replace 'stem' with 'tree', and this one will sound quite familiar to English speakers! German speakers use this idiom when comparing the similarities between a child and their parent.

- ***Es regnet in Strömen.*** *(It rains in streams.)*
- No, it doesn't rain cats and dogs in Germany when it rains heavily. Instead, *it rains in streams* which makes... a bit more sense, depending on who you're talking to.

- ***Es ist alles in Butter!*** *(Everything is in butter.)*
- Grease makes everything work smoothly. And for those that eat dairy, butter is a beautiful thing. This idiom can help you express that everything is great. Life is good.

- ***Ich habe zwei linke Hände.*** *(I have two left hands.)*
- When you're feeling less than talented at what you're doing, it would be appropriate to say that you have two left hands. You can also use this to describe a general clumsiness.

- ***Seine Zunge im Zaum halten.*** *(Keeping one's tongue in the bridle.)*
- If you need to hold back words or avoid answering in a spiteful way, then bite your tongue and remember this German saying.

- ***Da wird ja der Hund in der Pfanne verrückt!*** *(The dog in the pan gets crazy!)*
- If you see something totally out of the ordinary or hard to comprehend, this would be the expression to use in German.

- ***Ich stehe auf dem Schlauch*** (*I am standing on the hose.*)
- If you hear someone say this expression, get ready to offer help. The speaker does not know what to do or how to solve the problem at hand.

- ***Mit jemandem ist nicht gut Kirschen essen***
- Literally, this means 'It's not good to eat cherries with someone.' You would say this if someone is difficult to get along with.

- ***Angsthase***
- Is someone being a scaredy-cat? You might usc this German phrase instead, which translates to 'fear rabbit'.

- ***Um den heißen Brei herumreden***
- Avoiding an awkward conversation? Instead of ignoring the elephant in the room, or beating around the bush, you could say this phrase, which translates to 'to talk around the hot porridge'.

- ***Ich verstehe nur Bahnhof***
- The next time you mean to say 'it's all Greek to me', try this phrase instead. It translates to 'I only understand train station' and means that something is difficult to understand.

- ***Seinen Senf dazu geben***
- Looking for someone to share his thoughts? Instead of asking him to share his two cents, use this phrase to ask them to share their mustard.

- ***Jemandem die Daumen drücken***
- The next time you want to wish someone luck, instead of saying you'll keep your fingers crossed, try this German idiom—which means you'll press your thumbs.

- ***Ich bin fix und fertig!***
- Long day? Use this phrase to say you are 'quick and done', or exhausted.

- *Das ist ein Katzensprung.*
- This phrase literally means 'that's a cat's jump' and you can use it to say something is nearby.

- *Tomaten auf den Augen haben*
- Try this the next time someone is oblivious to what's going on. It literally means 'to have tomatoes on your eyes'.

- *Zwei Fliegen mit einer Klappe schlagen*
- Heading to a Biergarten to practice your German and make new friends? You might say you're 'hitting two flies with one swatter', or accomplishing two tasks at once.

GOING TO A RESTAURANT IN GERMANY

Going to a restaurant in a country where German is the primary language and sampling some of the delectable regional specialties is sure to be one of the most delightful cultural experiences you can have there.

When dining out, the following words will cover all the questions and comments you need to ask and make, from requesting a table to paying the bill!

Let's look at some of the basic vocabulary to order and have a fun dine-out experience in Germany:
- *Ein Tisch für eine Person bitte* – A table for one, please
- *Ein Tisch für zwei Personen, bitte* – A table for two, please
- **Haben Sie schon auf?** – Are you open yet?
- *Können wir (auf einen Tisch) warten?* – Can we wait (for a table)?
- *Können wir dort sitzen?* – Can we sit over there?
- *Entschuldigung!* – Excuse me! [Calling a waiter]
- *Was empfehlen Sie?* – What do you recommend?
- *Was ist das beliebteste Gericht?* – What's your most popular dish?
- *Was ist das?* – What is this?
- *Was für Bier haben Sie?* – What type of beer do you have?
- *Ein kleines Bier bitte* – A small beer, please
- *Ein großes Bier bitte* – A large beer, please

- *Bringen Sie mir bitte eine Auswahl von leckeren Sachen* – Please bring me a selection of nice things
- *Bitte wählen Sie etwas* – It's up to you / You can decide
- *Die Rechnung, bitte* – The bill, please
- *Kann ich bitte die Speisekarte haben?* – Can I have the menu, please?

TRANSPORT AND GETTING OUT AND ABOUT IN GERMANY

While planning a trip to Germany, there are many different practical aspects to think about, including how you will get around the country. It is not always easy to find the correct train or bus at the appropriate moment, and you do not want to end up as the 'foreigner' or 'Ausländer' who is holding up the ticket queue!

Now you will learn some key terms related to various modes of transportation, which will assist you in swiftly and effortlessly navigating your way around any city or country in which German is spoken:

- *Ich möchte nach _____* – I want to go to
- *Wann fährt der nächste Zug / Bus nach _____?* – What time is the next train/bus to ___?
- *Was kostet das?* – How much is it?
- *Einmal/ zweimal (nach _____), bitte* – 1 ticket / 2 tickets (to _____), please
- *Wie lange dauert das?* – How long does it take?
- *Wohin muss ich jetzt gehen?* – Where should I go now?
- *Wann fährt er ab?* – When does it leave?
- *Wie spät ist es (jetzt)?* – What time is it (now)?
- *Hält der Zug/ Bus in _?* – Does this train/bus stop in _____?
- *Entschuldigen Sie, ist dies _____?* – Excuse me, is this _____ ? [Useful when you're on the bus / train and are not sure when to get off]
- *Können Sie das bitte für mich aufschreiben?* – Can you write that down for me?
- *Zeigen Sie mir das bitte auf der Karte?* – Can you show me on the map?
- *Wo ist _____ auf der Karte?* – Where is _____ on the map?

SHOPPING IN GERMANY!

You are going to have to make some purchases at some point or another, regardless of whether you are in a grocery store, a shopping center, or even at a local farmer's market!

And don't be afraid to dicker a little bit, just like you would in English. You can save some money by learning these sentences in German.

Have a look at these most commonly used phrases in German:
- *Das gefällt mir* – I like this
- *Was kostet das?* – How much is this?
- *Bitte wiederholen Sie das* – Can you say that again please?
- *Schreiben Sie das bitte für mich auf?* – Can you write that down for me?
- *Und wenn ich das alles kaufe?* – If I buy these together? [A useful way to knock the price down]
- *Das ist mir zu teuer* – it's too expensive for me
- *Geben Sie mir einen Rabatt?* – Can you give me a discount?
- *Ich suche nach _____* – I'm looking for a _____
- *Ich schaue mich nur um* – I'm just looking around
- *Danke, ich suche noch weiter* – Thank you, I'll keep looking [if you're getting hassled to buy something]
- *Moment, bitte* – Just a moment
- *Ja, bitte* – Yes, please
- *Nein, danke* – No, thanks

MEDICAL CARE IN GERMANY!

We truly hope that you will never have a need for the terms contained in this section! In spite of this, it is always beneficial to have a fundamental understanding of medical terminology so that you can respond appropriately in the event that you become ill or are involved in an accident.

Let's look at the phrases that will help you to be at ease in case of a medical emergency:

- *Können Sie mir bitte helfen?* – Can you help me, please?

- *Ich brauche einen Arzt* – I need to see a doctor
- *Es geht mir nicht gut* – I do not feel well
- *Es geht ihm/ihr nicht gut* – he / she does not feel well
- *Gibt es ein Krankenhaus in der Nähe?* – Is there a hospital near here?
- *Fahren Sie mich bitte zum Krankenhaus* – Take me to the hospital [To a taxi driver]
- *Es tut hier weh* – It hurts here [pointing to body part]
- **Ich brauche Medizin** – I need some medicine

RANDOM HELPFUL PHRASES IN GERMAN

Let's conclude off this topic by learning a few additional phrases that don't fit neatly into any one particular group. You should now be able to speak in a manner that is more kind and natural by now with the help of our **'German Phrasebook for Adult Beginners'**.

We have included a couple of questions that you can ask the locals in order to have a more genuine experience while in Germany. This will allow you to discover the hidden gems in their cities. Let's quickly have a look:

- *Es tut mir leid, Sie zu stören, aber...* – I'm sorry to bother you, but ...
- *Kann ich Sie schnell etwas fragen?* – Could I ask you something quickly?
- *Ich suche ein Restaurant mit gutem Essen hier in der Nähe* – I'm looking for a place with good food around here
- *Ich suche ein nettes Café in der Nähe* – I'm looking for a nice Cafe in the area
- *Wissen Sie etwas über _____?* – Do you know anything about _____?
- *Gibt es hier in der Nähe etwas Interessantes zu sehen?* – Is there anything interesting to see in this area?
- *Trotzdem danke* – Thank you anyway

LESEN MACHT SPAß!!

Ein Tag im Schwimmbad

Heute gehe ich mit meiner Mutter ins Schwimmbad. Es ist ein sehr heißer Tag und ich freue mich auf das kalte Wasser. Am Eingang kaufen wir Eintrittskarten. Eine Eintrittskarte kostet einen Euro fünfzig (1,50). Meine Mutter gibt der Kassiererin das Geld. Im Schwimmbad suchen wir uns einen schönen Platz. Die Sonne scheint mir ins

Gesicht, während ich über die Wiese laufe. Viele Kinder spielen auf der Wiese. Auf der Wiese liegen viele Decken und Handtücher. Die Besucher liegen auf den Decken in der Sonne. Meine Mutter legt auch eine Decke auf die Wiese, dann gehen wir zum Schwimmbecken. Ich dusche mich, dann springe ich endlich in das kühle Wasser. Das ist erfrischend. Am liebsten würde ich jeden Tag ins Schwimmbad gehen. Ich schwimme ein paar Runden und spiele mit meinen Freunden. Um sieben (7) Uhr schließt das Schwimmbad und wir müssen nach Hause. Ich bin traurig. Ich habe immer viel Spaß im Schwimmbad. Morgen will ich wieder ins Schwimmbad. Mama sagt, dass wir das machen können.

'A day at the swimming pool'

Today I am going to the swimming pool with my mother. It is a very hot day and I am looking forward to the cold water. We buy tickets at the entrance. One ticket costs one euro fifty (1.50). My mother gives the money to the cashier. In the swimming pool we look for a nice place. The sun shines on my face while I walk across the grass. Many children play on the grass. There are many blankets and towels on the grass. The visitors lie on the blankets in the sun. My mother also puts a blanket on the grass, then we go to the pool. I take a shower, then I finally jump into the cool water. It's refreshing. I would love to go to the pool every day. I swim a few laps and play with my friends. At seven (7) o'clock the pool closes and we have to go home. I feel sad. I always have a lot of fun in the pool. Tomorrow I want to come to the pool again. Mom says we can do that.'

Fragen

-   Auf was freust du dich im Schwimmbad?
-   Wie viel Geld kostet die Eintrittskarte?
-   Was legt deine Mutter auf die Wiese?
-   Was machst du, bevor du ins Becken springst?
-   Wann schließt das Schwimmbad?

WORTSCHATZ!

-   Das Schwimmbad – the pool
-   heiß – hot
-   sich freuen auf – to look forward to

- kalt – cold
- der Eingang – the entrance
- kaufen – to buy
- suchen – to search
- der Platz – the place
- das Gesicht – the face
- die Wiese – the meadow
- duschen – to take a shower
- springen – to jump
- erfrischend – refreshing
- schließen – to close
- traurig sein – to be sad

Well, this was all about the basic conversation starters in the German language and also how to use them in basic in various situations, now we hope you enjoyed this too, because we sure did!

Es war spaßig! Now shall we move forward to the next chapter in our book '**German Phrasebook for Adult Beginners**' and learn how to introduce us to the German way?

Sind Sie aufgeregt? Because we are, see you in **Kapitel 4** with the basic german cases and their prepositions**!**

Bis bald!

KEY TAKEAWAYS!

In this chapter we have learned about:
- The basic words and phrases of the German language have been the focus of our studies in this chapter.
- The various situations that can arise in German and the appropriate responses to take in each one.
- The phrases and circumstances that are most frequently encountered in people's day-to-day life.
- How to inquire about directions in Germany, how to place an order in Germany, how to handle a medical emergency in Germany, and so many other possible scenarios are covered.

- LESEN MACHT SPAß: Reading is enjoyable, and doing so will assist you in expanding your German vocabulary and enhancing your reading abilities.
- The Wortschatz part that comes after the reading passages will help you expand your vocabulary!

KAPITEL 4

Wer das ABC recht kann, hat die schwerste Arbeit getan.

'Hallo zusammen! Wie geht es Ihnen?'

Wie geht es Ihnen? We are sure you know this statement and the answer to this statement by now! *Oder?*

The fundamentals of the German language were presented in our book 1 **'Learn German for beginners'** and if you've been following along with us for the past month, you should already be very well versed in the language. Now we are here in **Kapitel 4**, and we will learn the cases in German language and how to use them with their prepositions in day-to-day lives!

We will talk about the basic vocabulary in German language that will help you in sounding like a Deutscher and also have a *LESEN MACHT SPAß* to enhance your German language skills.

We have been working so hard this past month, with our 30 days challenge, we are sure that with the help of our **'German Phrasebook for Adult Beginners'** you will also be fluent in German in no time!

Los geht's!

THE GERMAN CASES

Hallo, wie geht es Ihnen?

Before we get to the fun part, there is some fundamental information that we need to uncover, and that is the fact that German phrases, as well as their word sequence, are rather adaptable. The verb is the only thing that is as stable as the Leaning Tower of Pisa! It is located in the middle of the second clause of a sentence. Hence it is the focus of our **Kapitel 4** and we will learn more about that and the cases in our book **'German Phrasebook for Adult Beginners'**.

It's possible that if we mention again that, 'In English, the verb also comes second, after the subject', you would get bored and shrug. But, this is exactly the point: following the subject.

When writing in German, the topic of a sentence does not always need to come first in the sentence. The subject of a sentence is highlighted by the first position. Because this is the focus of attention, everyone wants their share of the spotlight during these moments. Because of this, you might begin your phrase with an object, such as in the following example:

Diesen schönen Kuchen hier werde ich jetzt essen. (I'm going to devour this delicious cake right now.)

Although while it may be pretty obvious here, who is eating who, there are situations in which it is not always this obvious, and we need the articles as the case marker to inform us what is the subject and what is the object of the sentence.

So, Fangen wir an! Los Gehts!

NOMINATIVE CASE

The first case in the German case system is called the ***nominative case***. It offers a description of the thing being discussed in the statement. Whenever and in every language, a sentence's subject specifies the person or object that is carrying out the action of the sentence.

Zum eispiel: *Der Mann ist nett.* (The man is a nice person.)

As can be seen, the gentleman is the one who is making an effort, and he has a pleasant attitude. So, all you have to do to inquire about the subject of your sentence is make use of the word **'wer'**, which is the inquiry word for who. You must remember this from the 'W' Fragen section from our previous book!

When inquiring about a topic that is not anything alive, the question 'was' (what) can also be asked in the classical German language.

For our example above, the question would be: ***Wer ist nett? Answer: Der Mann.***

Ich esse; I eat. Here, it is ich (*I*) who does the eating.

Der Stuhl bricht zusammen; The chair breaks down.

And here it is *der Stuhl* (the chair) that does the breaking down

Ich bin ein Eichhörnchen; I'm a squirrel.

You must be thinking that this case is very easy; first one is the subject, second one the object. But no, the verb 'to be' is the verbal form for an equation: 'Ich=Eichhörnchen' That's why, the 'Eichhörnchen' is a nominative, too.

Genders in Nominative

Defined article		Undefined article	
Male	der (the)	ein (a)	Der / ein Mann tanzt Tango.
Female	die (the)	eine (a)	Die / eine Frau isst einen Bagel.
Neuter	das (the)	ein (a)	Das / ein Kind spielt Basketball.
Plural	die (the)	/	Die / – Autos sind schön.

ACCUSATIVE CASE

When a noun functions as the direct object of a sentence, the **'accusative case'** is the one that is applied. In other words, when it is the subject of the action being described (also known as the 'verb') in the sentence.

When a noun is placed in the accusative case, the words for 'the' differ very slightly from those used when the noun is in the nominative case, ***zum Beispiel:***

- ***Der Mann findet <u>den Ball</u>.*** (The man finds the ball.)

Der Mann is the subject/nominative, while den Ball is the direct object/accusative. But this only happens with masculine nouns. Take a look at this second example that uses two feminine nouns (Frau, Blume):

- ***Die Frau findet <u>die Blume.</u>*** (The woman finds the flower.)

ACCUSATIVE CASE GENDERS (Direct object of the sentence)

Masculine der   den
neutral   das   das
Feminine die   die
Plural   die   die

When it comes to everything else apart from the masculine nouns, the word for 'the' is exactly the same whether it is used in the subject position (*nominative*) or the direct object position *(accusative)*.

PREPOSITIONS WITH ACCUSATIVE

Well to be clear, we have been using the accusative form for objects that are the direct object in a sentence, or for the thing that is being 'verbed'.

Yet, there is one more situation in which you will employ the accusative case. There are a few connectors or words known as prepositions that, wherever they are used, indicate that the accusative case should be used.

That is to say, if you come across any of these specific connectors or words in a phrase, the noun that comes following the term ought to be in the accusative case!

These are:

- Bis - until
- Durch - through
- Für - for
- Gegen - against
- Wieder - against (contrary to)
- Ohne - without
- Entlang - along
- Um - around

Let's look at some sentences that use these accusative prepositions and see what they look like:

- *Die Frau pflückt zwei Blumen **für den Mann**.* (The woman picked two flowers for the man.)

Because *für* is an accusative preposition, it indicates that the following noun in the phrase, which is der Mann, should also be in the accusative case. And because der Mann is a masculine noun, it turns to den Mann.

Is this easy enough? ***Ja? Gut!***

DATIVE CASE

When describing the indirect object of a sentence, the ***dative*** case is used. A noun that is the receiver of something is called an indirect object (usually the direct accusative object). In German, this concept is referred to as der Dativ.

In this specific case, the questions, 'wem?' (meaning 'to whom?') and 'was?' (meaning 'what?') are answered.

The German Definite Articles in Dative Case

When it is assumed that the reader or listener is familiar with the subject being discussed, a definite article is used before the noun. Often, it refers to a particular person or thing that is being discussed. The word 'the' functions as a definite article in English. Zum Beispiel: The man is suffering from a cold. Here, a specific man is suffering from a cold.

To fully comprehend the dative case, there is one more part that must be added:
Who or what is being passively received the action or is simply kind of hanging out in the sentence, doing nothing? This is an example of an indirect object.

- Subject (Who/what does the action?)
- Verb (The action)
- Direct object (What is being 'verbed')
- the accordion (the accordion is being played)
- Indirect object (What is passively receiving the action, or just kind of hanging out?)

You are already aware that when referring to the subject of a sentence, we use the nominative case, and when referring to the direct object of a statement, we use the accusative case. If there is an indirect object in a sentence, then that object must be in the dative case. Zum Beispiel:

- *The man reads a book to the children*

    The man is Nominative, the book is Accusative and the children are Dative.

ACHTUNG!!

Remember how indirect objects simply kind of hang out in the sentence while something else or someone else does all the work? Well, that's the catch for you to remember the Dative case!

GENDER IN DATIVE CASE

Masculine	der	dem
Feminine	die	der
Neutral	das	dem
Plural	die	den

Let's have a look at some of the Dative prepositions:
- Aus - from
- Außer - except for
- Bei - with/ by
- Mit - with
- Nach - after/to
- Seit - since/ for
- Von - from/of
- Zu - to

GENITIVE CASE

The final and least frequently used German case is the genitive. In everyday speech and writing, the dative case almost always takes its place.

You should know that the Genitive case is not commonly used and you can easily handle everyday scenarios just fine without it. But this is also a very important part of the German language and so, we will learn about it too!

Secondly, keep in mind that the four situations describe the function that each noun serves in a phrase and, consequently, how each word connects to the other nouns.

So what is the Genitive case?

In both English and German, the genitive case denotes a connection between two nouns. In the genitive case, the noun modifies (explains) the other noun. The first noun is a component of, associated with, a member of, or dependent upon the genitive case noun, zum Besipiel:

- Das Auto **des Vaters.**
- Die Regeln der Schule.

How German Genitive Case Works

German, broadly defined, uses the same two genitive constructions, and the timing of when to apply each one is actually rather close to English as well! *Geil*!

German has two ways to form the genitive:

- Add an 's' (no apostrophe!)
- Use the structure: modified noun + determiner (and/or +adjectives) + modifying noun

If a name or a phrase for a family member is listed immediately in front of the noun that it modifies in German, then we can add an's' to the end of the name without using an apostrophe, zum Beispiel:

- Vaters Handy
- Opas Katze

GENDER IN GENITIVE CASE

Masculine	der	des
Feminine	die	der
Neutral	das	des
Plural	die	der

KEY TAKEAWAYS!

In this chapter we have covered:

- The three basic cases of the German language
- The prepositions of the cases and examples to use them
- The nominative case and its explanation
- The accusative case and its explanation
- The Genitive case and its explanation

SCHLUSSFOLGERUNG/ CONCLUSION

Ach, endlich! This book provides a glimpse into the German cases, and we really hope that going through them was as enjoyable for the readers as it was for the authors to do so. *Ist das so?*

We went to great lengths to make sure that the ideas presented in the book may be comprehended easily by anyone who reads it; we hope that our efforts were successful. To broaden your horizons even more, there are also fairly basic translations offered wherever they are required.

Well, *wie war das?* How did things turn out with the German cases? *Wir hoffen, sie waren nicht zu viel für Sie!* (We hope that they weren't too much for you to handle)

You can learn to master the German cases by practicing recognizing them in German writings and stories. Cases can be found anywhere; all you have to do is look for them.

Moving on to some more advanced topics, let's talk about some German short stories now that we've covered some of the fundamentals. Not only will you make progress in your *Sprache* by doing this, but you'll also have a good time doing it! See you in our next book!

Bis bald!!

BOOK 3

German Short Stories for Adult Beginners: Become Conversational Today with Fun & Engaging Stories!

Shortcut Your Fluency in German!

Fun & Easy Stories

INTRODUCTION

~Neue Bücher, neue Lehre

'Hallo zusammen! Wie geht es Ihnen?'

Before we get into German stories, let us tell you our happiness that you are here, continuing, or starting your journey to fluent German. We know how hard it is to learn German, and we hope this book will help you get closer to your goals, help you with the vocabulary and in no time you will be the master of German, thanks to our German **Short Stories for Adult Beginners: Become Conversational Today with Fun & Engaging Stories!**

The process of mastering a new language is similar to **Kochen**; it requires a lot of Ü**bung**, as well as the correct preparation, time and cooking methods, but the finished dish will be l**ecker**!

Learning German is not **einfach**, but we have tried to make it easier for you with this book. Because German is flexible and there are so many words which you should know, we compiled this collection of German short stories to help you learn the language. With the help of stories, you can enhance your H**ören** (hearing), experiencing the words on your tongue and their **Sprechen** (pronunciation), and **Lesen** (reading).

These short stories are ideal for those just starting out with the German language. Reading easy and fun stories is the most effective way to learn German without leaving the country and taking a trip to Germany.

This collection of short stories features conversations between people dealing with everyday challenges, utilizing the most useful phrases and expressions in German language.

With that in mind, we set out to write a book aimed at the beginning level of the reader. The language is straightforward without becoming too tough to understand or dull. The majority of the book is written in the present tense, making it easier to observe conversations, learn and understand verb roots, and recognize patterns in the book's subject verb agreements.

Short Stories for Adult Beginners: Become Conversational Today with Fun & Engaging Stories is the book you should read to master your German. The stories are easy to follow, but not oversimplified. While not being intended for young readers, the language is straightforward enough for novices to understand.

Los geht's!!

Aber zuerst, warum und wie?

Learning more words in German

What better way than the stories which we have handpicked for you in our '**Short Stories for Adult Beginners: Become Conversational Today with Fun & Engaging Stories**' to learn new words and expand your vocabulary?

Books are made of words, words, and more words! It is only natural, then, that many students of German who decide they wish to enhance their vocabularies do so by first visiting a bookstore.

In addition, finding a book in German on a topic of interest will make it simple to pick up new vocabulary words. To learn more about the German language and enhance your vocabulary, read a story from the many different types of stories given in our book, ***Super! Oder?***

Grammatik!

German words are not used alone & outside of dictionaries. Here's when proper grammar comes into play! Reading in German is an excellent approach to master the German language's grammar, provided you pay close attention to the construction of the sentences. You may even learn everything there is to know about German vowels and how to pronounce them.

Learning to Pronounce Properly

A good way to improve your German pronunciation is to listen to a German audiobook, especially if you prefer listening to reading. Listening to the book is a great way to passively learn more about German dialects and pronunciation. A more useful approach would be to repeat after the narrator in an effort to imitate his accent. Reading aloud from paper books is another effective way for students to refine their German pronunciation.

KAPITEL 1

Wie soll einer lehrfähig sein, wenn er nicht mehr lernfähig ist?

The Mysterious Package / Greetings

HANDLUNG

Es klingelt an der Tür.

Andrew läuft zur Tür der Wohnung. Die Türklingel klingelt am Samstagmorgen nie. Andrew freut sich, zu sehen, wer an der Tür ist. Er öffnet die Tür.

'Guten Morgen, kleiner Junge', sagt ein Bote. Der Mann ist in einer braunen Uniform gekleidet und trägt eine braune Schachtel.

'Hallo, der Herr', sagt Andrew.

'Ich habe ein Paket', sagt der Lieferant, 'für die Hauptstraße 10'.

'Das ist die Hauptstraße 10', sagt Andrew.

'Das Paket hat keinen Namen', sagt der Lieferant, 'es hat auch keine Wohnungsnummer.

'Wie seltsam!' sagt Andrew.

Kannst du es der richtigen Person geben?' fragt der Mann.

'Ich kann es versuchen', sagt Andrew. Er ist erst zehn Jahre alt, aber er fühlt sich wichtig.

'Vielen Dank', sagt der Lieferant. Er geht, Andrew bringt die Schachtel in sein Haus. Er starrt auf die Schachtel.

Sie hat ungefähr die Größe eines Schuhkartons. Auf dem Paket steht kein Name, nur Hauptstraße 10.

Andrew öffnet den Pappkarton. Er muss wissen, was drin ist, um den Besitzer zu finden. In dem Pappkarton befindet sich eine kleine Holzkiste. Andrew öffnet die Holzkiste. In der Kiste sind 10 verschiedene Brillenpaare.

Sie haben unterschiedliche Farben: rosa und rot, grüne Pünktchen, schwarz und weiß. Sie haben auch unterschiedliche Formen: rund, quadratisch und rechteckig.

Er schließt die Schachtel und zieht seine Schuhe an.

'Tschüss , Mama! 'Ich bin gleich wieder da', schreit er.

Andrew klopft an die Tür gegenüber seiner Wohnung. Sie öffnet sich. Eine sehr alte Dame lächelt Andrew mit seiner Schachtel an.

'Guten Morgen, Frau Smith!' sagt Andrew.

Wie geht es dir?' fragt die alte Dame.

'Gut, danke! Und Ihnen?' fragt Andrew.

'Was hast du da?' fragte die alte Dame.

'Fräulein', das ist ein Paket. 'Es gehört jemandem in diesem Gebäude, aber ich weiß nicht wem', sagt Andrew.

'Es ist nicht für mich', sagt die alte Dame. 'Unmöglich!'

'Oh, okay' sagt Andrew, enttäuscht. Die alte Dame trägt eine Brille. Er denkt sich, dass die Brillen ihr gut stehen würden. Er dreht sich um, zu gehen.

'Komm später wieder', ruft die alte Dame, 'ich mache Kekse und ein paar Kekse sind für dich und deine Familie.'

Andrew geht die Treppe hoch. Sein Gebäude hat 2 Etagen. Er ist mit fast jedem im Gebäude befreundet. Allerdings hat die Wohnung im ersten Stock eine neue Familie. Andrew kennt sie nicht. Er ist schüchtern, aber er klingelt. Ein braunhaariger Mann öffnet die Tür, er lächelt.

'Hallo!' sagt der Mann.

'Hallo', sagt Andrew, 'ich wohne unten, mein Name ist Andrew.'

'Schön, dich kennenzulernen, Andrew', sagt der Mann. 'Wir sind neu im Haus, ich bin Herr Jones.'

'Freut mich auch, Sie kennenzulernen', sagt Andrew. 'Dieses Paket gehört jemandem in diesem Gebäude. Ist es Ihr Paket?'

'Unmöglich!' sagt der Mann. Meine Familie und ich sind gerade erst hergezogen. Niemand kennt unsere Adresse.'

'Okay', sagt Andrew. 'Schön, Sie kennenzulernen.' Die Tür schließt sich. Ein weiteres Nein. Es sind nur noch zwei weitere Wohnungen übrig.

Es gibt noch eine weitere Wohnung, die Wohnung im zweiten Stock. Herr Edwards lebt allein in dieser Wohnung. Er hat einen großen Papagei, der weiß, wie man redet. Er hat auch vier Katzen und einen Hund. Seine Wohnung ist alt und dunkel. Andrew hat Angst vor Herr Edwards. Er klingelt an der Tür. Er muss herausfinden, wem das Paket gehört

Hallo,'sagt Herr Edwards. Sein Hund kommt zur Tür. Der Hund hilft Herr Edwards, da er blind ist.

'Hallo, Herr Edwards. 'Ich bin es, Andrew', sagt Andrew. Herr Edwards hat die Augen geschlossen, er lächelt.

'Was gibt es Neues, Andrew?' fragte er. Hmmm, denkt Andrew, vielleicht ist Herr Edwards nicht furchterregend. Vielleicht ist Herr Edwards nur ein netter alter Mann, der allein lebt.

'Ich habe ein Paket und ich denke, es ist für Sie', sagt Andrew.

'Oh ja! Meine Lesebrillen, endlich!'lächelt Herr Edwards. Er streckt seine Hände aus. Andrew ist verwirrt. Er sieht den Hund an. Er scheint auch zu lächeln. Er gibt Herr Edwards die Schachtel.

'Schön, dich zu sehen.', sagt Herr Edwards.

'Sie auch!', sagt Andrew. Vielleicht besucht er Herr Edwards wieder an einen anderen Tag. Er dreht sich um und geht nach Hause.

ÜBERSETZUNG/ TRANSLATION

The doorbell rings.

Andrew runs to the door of the apartment. The doorbell never rings on Saturday morning. Andrew is happy to see who is at the door. He opens the door.

'Good morning, little boy,' says the messenger. The man is dressed in a brown uniform and carries a brown box.

'Hello, sir,' says Andrew.

'I have a package,' says the delivery man, 'for 10 Main Street.'

'This is 10 Main Street,' says Andrew.

'The parcel has no name,' says the delivery man, 'nor does it have an apartment number.'

'How strange!' says Andrew.

'Can you give it to the right person?' asks the man.

'I can try,' says Andrew. He's only ten years old, but he feels important.

'Thank you very much,' says the delivery man. He leaves, Andrew takes the box to his house. He stares at the box. It's about the size of a shoebox. There is no name on the package, just 10 Main Street.

Andrew opens the cardboard box. He needs to know what is inside to find the owner. Inside the cardboard box is a small wooden box. Andrew opens the wooden box. In the box there are 10 different pairs of glasses. They have different colors: pink and red, green dots, black and white. They also have different shapes: round, square and rectangular.

He closes the box and puts on his shoes.

'Bye, Mom! 'I'll be right back,' he yells.

Andrew knocks on the door opposite his apartment. It opens. A very old lady smiles at Andrew with his box.

'Good morning, Mrs Smith!' says Andrew.

'How are you ?' asks the old lady.

'Fine, thank you! And you ?' asks Andrew.

'What have you got there ?' asks the old lady.

'Miss', it's a package. 'It belongs to someone in this building, but I don't know who,' says Andrew.

'It's not for me,' says the old lady. 'Impossible!'

'Oh, okay,' says Andrew, disappointed. The old lady is wearing glasses. He thinks to himself that glasses would look good on her. He turns to leave.

'Come back later,' the old lady calls, 'I'm making cookies, and some cookies are for you and your family.'

Andrew walks up the stairs. His building has 2 floors. He is friends with almost everyone in the building. However, the second floor apartment has a new family. Andrew doesn't know them. He is shy, but he rings the doorbell. A brown-haired man opens the door, smiling.

'Hello!' the man says.

'Hello,' says Andrew, 'I live downstairs, my name is Andrew.'

'Nice to meet you, Andrew,' says the man. 'We're new to the house, I'm Mr. Jones.'

'Nice to meet you too,' says Andrew. 'This package belongs to someone in this building. Is it your package?'

'Impossible!' says the man. 'My family and I just moved here. Nobody knows our address.'

'Okay,' says Andrew.' Nice to meet you.' The door closes. Another No. There are only two more apartments left.

There is one more apartment, the second floor apartment. Mr. Edwards lives alone in this apartment. He has a big parrot that knows how to talk. He also has four cats and a dog. His apartment is old and dark. Andrew is afraid of Mr. Edwards. He rings the doorbell. He has to find out who the package belongs to

Hello,' says Mr. Edwards. His dog comes to the door. The dog helps Mr. Edwards because he is blind.

'Hello, Mr. Edwards. 'It's Andrew,' says Andrew. Mr. Edwards has his eyes closed, he smiles.

'What's new, Andrew?' he asked. Hmm, thinks Andrew, maybe Mr. Edwards is not scary. Maybe Mr. Edwards is just a nice old man who lives alone.

'I have a package and I think it's for you,' says Andrew.

'Oh yes! My reading glasses, at last!' smiles Mr. Edwards. He holds out his hands. Andrew is confused. He looks at the dog. He seems to be smiling, too. He hands the box to Mr. Edwards.

'Good to see you,' says Mr. Edwards.

'You too!' says Andrew. Perhaps he will visit Mr. Edwards again on another day. He turns around and goes home.

ZUSAMMENFASSUNG/ SUMMARY

Andrew, a boy, gets a parcel that wasn't intended for him. A carton of glasses is inside. To find out who the parcel belongs to, he takes it to each of his neighbors one by one. It comes as a slight surprise to him to learn that the parcel belongs to his next-door neighbor, Mr. Edwards.

WORTSCHATZ!

guten Morgen	Good morning
Hallo	Hello
Herr	Sir
vielen Dank	Thank you very much
Tschüss	Bye
Guten Morgen!	Morning!
Wie geht es dir?	How are you?
In Ordnung, danke schön! Und was ist mit dir?	Fine, thanks! And you?
Mein Name ist...	My Name is...

Freut mich, dich kennenzulernen	It's nice to meet you
Wie läuft es so?	How's it going?
Freut mich auch, Sie kennenzulernen	Nice to meet you too
Es geht so	It's going
Hallo	Hey
Wie läuft es denn so	What's up
Schön, dich zu sehen	It's good to see you!

FRAGEN

Wählen Sie nur eine Antwort pro Frage aus.

1. Wer ist an der Haustür, wenn Andrew sie öffnet?

a) ein Lieferant

b) eine Katze

c) ein Volkszähler

d) sein Vater

2. Wie würden Sie Frau Smith beschreiben?

a) ein schönes Mädchen

b) eine gemeine Person

c) ein schlechter Nachbar

d) eine nette alte Frau

3. Wer wohnt im ersten Stock des Wohnhauses?

a) niemand

b) ein Mädchen aus Andrews Schule

c) eine neue Familie

d) Andrew

4. Wem gehören die Brillen im Haus?

a) der alten Frau

b) dem blinden Mann

c) Andrew und seiner Familie

d) niemandem

ANTWORTEN

1. Wer ist an der Haustür, wenn Andrew sie öffnet?

a) ein Lieferant

2. Wie würdest du Frau Smith beschreiben?

d) eine nette alte Frau

3. Wer wohnt im ersten Stock des Wohnhauses?

c) eine neue Familie

4. Wem gehören die Brillen im Haus?

b) dem blinden Mann

ENGLISCH!

1. Who is at the front door when Andrew opens it?

a) a deliveryman

2) How would you describe Mrs. Smith?

d) a nice old woman

3. Who lives on the second floor of the apartment building?

c) a new family

4. Who owns the glasses in the house?

b) the blind man

KAPITEL 2

'Das Ziel der Wünsche steht niemals still.'
von George Gerhard Reisenberg

MARDI GRAS

HANDLUNG

Frank tritt aus seiner Haustür. Sein neues Haus ist violett, mit blauen Fenstern. Die Farben sind sehr hell für ein Haus. In New Orleans, seinem neuen Zuhause, sind Gebäude bunt.

Er ist neu in der Nachbarschaft. Frank hat noch keine Freunde. Das Haus neben ihm ist ein großes, rotes Gebäude. Eine Familie lebt dort. Frank starrt die Tür an, als ein Mann sie öffnet. Frank grüßt ihn.

'Hallo, Nachbar!' sagt George. Er winkt, Frank geht zum roten Haus.

'Hallo, ich bin Frank, der neue Nachbar', sagt Frank.

'Schön, dich kennenzulernen, mein Name ist George', sagt George. Die Männer schütteln sich die Hände. George hat eine Lichterkette in den Händen. Die Lichter sind grün, lila und golden.

'Wofür sind die Lichter?' fragte Frank.

'Du bist neu', lacht George. 'Es ist Mardi Gras, wusstest du das nicht? Diese Farben repräsentieren den Karnevalsfeiertag hier in New Orleans.'

'Oh, ja,'sagt Frank. Frank weiß nichts über Mardi Gras. Er hat auch keine Freunde, mit denen er Pläne machen kann.

'Heute ist Freitag ', sagt George. Es gibt eine Parade namens Endymion. Wirst du mit mir und meiner Familie hingehen und zuschauen?'

'Ja,' sagt Frank. 'Wunderbar!'

George macht die Lichter an das Haus, Frank hilft George, George macht das Licht an, das Haus sieht festlich aus.

Die Familie und Frank gehen zur Parade. Während des Mardi Gras gibt es in New Orleans jeden Tag Paraden. Die Paraden während der Woche sind klein. Die Paraden am Wochenende, Samstag und Sonntag, sind groß, mit vielen Festwagen und Menschen. Es gibt einen König des Mardi Grases. Sein Name ist Rex.

Mardi Gras bedeutet Faschings-Dienstag. In England heißt es Fastnachtsdienstag. Der Feiertag ist katholisch. Es ist ein Tag vor Aschermittwoch, der Beginn der Fastenzeit. Mardi Gras ist die Feier vor der Fastenzeit, einer ernsten Zeit.

Ab Donnerstag sind die besonderen Tage vorbei. New Orleans ist berühmt für sein Mardi Gras. Menschen feiern und tragen Masken und Kostüme. Tatsächlich kann man eine Maske in New Orleans nur zu Mardi Gras tragen. Den Rest des Jahres ist es illegal!

George und seine Familie sehen mit Frank zu, wie die Parade beginnt. Frank ist überrascht. Viele Leute sehen zu, sie stehen im Gras. Festwagen passieren die Gruppe. Festwagen sind große Strukturen mit Menschen und Dekorationen. Sie gehen die Straße hinunter, einer nach dem anderen.

Der erste Festwagen repräsentiert die Sonne. Er hat gelbe Verzierungen. Eine Frau in der Mitte trägt ein weißes Kleid. Sie sieht aus wie ein Engel. Sie wirft den Leuten orangefarbene Spielzeuge und Perlen zu.

'Warum wirft sie Spielsachen und Halsketten?', fragt Frank.

'Für uns!' sagt Hannah, Georges Frau.

Hannah hält fünf Halsketten in ihren Händen. Einige Perlen liegen auf dem Boden. Niemand fängt sie auf. Sie sind schmutzig und braun.

Die Parade geht weiter. Es gibt viele Festwagen und viele Perlen. George und seine Familie rufen: 'Wirf etwas her, Meister!'Hannah füllt ihre schwarze Tasche mit bunten Spielzeugen und Perlen aus den Festwagen. Frank lernt 'Wirf mir etwas zu' zu schreien, um Perlen für sich selbst zu bekommen.

Einer der großen Festwagen hat über 250 Personen. Er ist der größte der Welt.

Schließlich endet die Parade. Die Kinder und die Erwachsenen sind glücklich. Jeder geht nach Hause, Frank ist müde. Er ist außerdem hungrig und will essen. Er folgt George und seiner Familie ins rote Haus.

Auf dem Tisch steht ein großer, runder Kuchen. Er sieht aus wie ein Ring, mit einem Loch in der Mitte. Auf dem Kuchen befinden sich lila , grüne und gelbe Glasur.

'Das ist Dreikönigskuchen', sagt Hannah. 'Wir essen jeden Mardi Gras Dreikönigskuchen.'

Hannah schneidet ein Stück Kuchen, sie gibt ein Stück George, ein Stück den Kindern und ein Stück Frank. Frank probiert den Kuchen. Es ist köstlich! Es schmeckt wie Zimt, es ist weich, aber plötzlich beißt Frank in Plastik.

'Aua!' sagt Frank. Frank hört auf zu essen, er zieht ein Plastikbaby aus dem Kuchen.

'Es gibt noch eine weitere Tradition', sagt George.

'Der Kuchen hat ein Baby in sich, die Person, die das Baby bekommt, kauft den nächsten Kuchen.'

'Das bin ich!' sagt Frank.

Alle lachen. George lädt Frank zu einer weiteren Parade am Montag ein.

Frank geht glücklich nach Hause. Er liebt Mardi Gras.

ÜBERSETZUNG/ TRANSLATION

Frank steps out of his front door. His new house is purple with blue windows. The colors are very bright for a house. In New Orleans, his new home, buildings are colorful.

He is new to the neighborhood. Frank doesn't have any friends yet. The house next to him is a big red building. A family lives there. Frank stares at the door as a man opens it. Frank greets him.

'Hello, neighbor!'says George. He waves, Frank goes to the red house.

'Hi, I'm Frank, the new neighbor,' Frank says.

'Nice to meet you, my name is George,' says George. The men shake hands. George has a string of lights in his hands. The lights are green , purple and gold .

'What are the lights for?' asked Frank.

'You're new,' George laughs. 'It's Mardi Gras, didn't you know?' Those colors represent the Mardi Gras holiday here in New Orleans.'

'Oh, yeah,'says Frank. Frank doesn't know anything about Mardi Gras. He also has no friends to make plans with.

'Today is Friday,' George says. 'There's a parade called Endymion. Will you go with me and my family and watch?'

'Yes,' says Frank. 'Wonderful!'

George puts the lights on the house, Frank helps George, George puts the lights on, the house looks festive.

The family and Frank go to the parade. During Mardi Gras, there are parades every day in New Orleans. The parades during the week are small. The parades on the weekend, Saturday and Sunday, are big, with lots of floats and people. There is a king of Mardi Gras. His name is Rex.

Mardi Gras means Mardi Gras Tuesday. In England it is called Shrove Tuesday. The holiday is Catholic. It is a day before Ash Wednesday, the beginning of Lent. Mardi Gras is the celebration before Lent, a serious time.

As of Thursday, the special days are over. New Orleans is famous for its Mardi Gras. People celebrate and wear masks and costumes. In fact, you can only wear a mask in New Orleans during Mardi Gras. The rest of the year it is illegal!

George and his family watch with Frank as the parade begins. Frank is surprised. Many people are watching, standing in the grass. Floats pass the group. Floats are large structures with people and decorations. They go down the street, one by one.

The first float represents the sun. It has yellow decorations. A woman in the middle is wearing a white dress. She looks like an angel. She throws orange toys and beads to the people.

'Why is she throwing toys and necklaces?' asks Frank.

'For us!' says Hannah, George's wife.

Hannah holds five necklaces in her hands. Some beads are on the floor. No one is catching them. They are dirty and brown .

The parade goes on. There are many floats and many beads. George and his family shout, 'Throw me something, master!' Hannah fills her black bag with colorful toys and beads from the floats. Frank learns to shout 'Throw me something' to get beads for himself.

One of the big floats has over 250 people. It is the largest in the world.

Finally, the parade ends. The children and the adults are happy. Everyone goes home, Frank is tired. He is also hungry and wants to eat. He follows George and his family into the red house.

There is a big round cake on the table. It looks like a ring, with a hole in the middle. On the cake are purple , green and yellow icing.

'This is Epiphany cake,' Hannah says. 'We eat Epiphany cake every Mardi Gras.'

Hannah cuts a piece of cake, she gives a piece to George, a piece to the kids and a piece to Frank. Frank tries the cake. 'It's delicious! It tastes like cinnamon, it's soft, but suddenly Frank bites into plastic.

'Ouch!' says Frank. Frank stops eating, he pulls a plastic baby out of the cake.

'There's another tradition,' George says.

'The cake has a baby in it, the person who gets the baby buys the next cake.'

'That's me!'says Frank.

Everyone laughs. George invites Frank to another parade on Monday.

Frank goes home happy. He loves Mardi Gras.

ZUSAMMENFASSUNG/ SUMMARY

Frank is new to New Orleans and his new house is purple with blue windows. The house next to him is a red building and a man opens the door. Frank greets him and the man introduces himself to George. George has a string of lights in his hands and explains that they are for the Mardi Gras holiday in New Orleans. Frank and his family go to the parade and George puts the lights on the house.

The parade is a day before Ash Wednesday, the beginning of Lent, and people celebrate and wear masks and costumes. George and his family watch with Frank as the parade ends. The first float in the Mardi Gras parade is a woman in a white dress who throws orange toys and beads to the people. George and his family shout, 'Throw me something, master!' Hannah fills her black bag with colorful toys and beads from the floats, and Frank learns to shout 'Throw me something' to get beads for himself.

The parade ends and everyone goes home, but Frank is hungry and wants to eat. Hannah gives him a big round cake with purple, green and yellow icing, and George invites Frank to another parade on Monday, and Frank goes home happy.

WORTSCHATZ!

Violett	Violet
Rot	Red
Farben	Colors
Blau	Blue
Grün	Green
Lila	purple
Gold	gold
Gelb	Yellow
Freitag	Friday
Woche	Week

Montag	Monday
Samstag	Saturday
Sonntag	Sunday
Dienstag	Tuesday
Mittwoch	Wednesday
Donnerstag	Thursday
Weiß	White
Orange	Orange
Braun	Brown
Schwarz	Black

FRAGEN

Wählen Sie nur eine Antwort pro Frage aus.

1. Wie würden Sie Franks neues Haus beschreiben?

a) langweilig

b) farbenfroh

c) winzig

d) einsam

2. Welche Farbe repräsentiert Mardi Gras in New Orleans?

a) blau

b) weiß

c) orange

d) Gold

3. Mardi Gras ist eine Feier:

a) nur für Erwachsene.

b) aus der Tradition der jüdischen Gemeide.

c) in New Orleans berühmt.

d) die man zu Hause feiert.

4. Was davon ist nicht auf einem Karnevalswagen?

a) Menschen

b) Computer

c) Spielzeug

d) Perlen

5. Was passiert, wenn Sie das Baby in einem Dreikönigskuchen finden?

a) Sie weinen

b) Sie müssen sich um das Baby kümmern

c) geben es Ihrem Freund

d) Sie müssen einen Königskuchen kaufen

ANTWORTEN

1. Wie würden Sie Franks neues Haus beschreiben?

a) Farbenfroh

2. Welche Farbe repräsentiert Mardi Gras in New Orleans?

d) Gold

3. Mardi Gras ist eine Feier:

c) in New Orleans berühmt.

4. Was davon ist nicht auf einem Karnevalswagen?

b) Computer

5. Was passiert, wenn Sie das Baby in einem Dreikönigskuchen finden?

d) Sie müssen einen Dreikönigskuchen kaufen.

ENGLISCH

1. How would you describe Frank's new house?

a) colorful

2. Which color represents Mardi Gras in New Orleans?

d) gold

3. Mardi Gras is a celebration:

(c) famous in New Orleans.

4. which of these is not on a Mardi Gras float?

b) computer

5. What happens if you find the baby in an Epiphany cake?

d) You must buy an Epiphany cake.

KAPITEL 3

Man erstickt den Verstand der Kinder unter
einem Ballast unnützer Kenntnisse
von Voltaire

SONDERBARES WETTER

HANDLUNG

Ivan ist zwölf Jahre alt. Er besucht seine Großeltern am Wochenende. Er liebt es, seine Großeltern zu besuchen. Oma gibt ihm jeden Tag Kekse und Milch. Opa bringt ihm tolle Sachen bei. Dieses Wochenende geht er zu ihnen.

Es ist Februar. Wo Ivan ist, ist Winter. Im Februar schneit es gewöhnlich. Ivan liebt den Schnee. Er spielt darin und rollt ihn zu Bällen. Dieses Februarwochenende ist das Wetter anders. Die Sonne scheint; es ist sonnig und fast heiß! Ivan trägt ein T-Shirt zum Haus seiner Großeltern.

'Hi, Opa! Hi, Oma!'sagt Ivan. 'Hallo, Ivan!'sagt Oma.

'Ivan! Wie geht's dir?' fragt Opa.

'Mir geht es gut', sagt er und umarmt seine Großeltern. Ivan verabschiedet sich von seiner Mutter.

Sie gehen ins Haus. 'Dieses Wetter ist seltsam', sagt Oma. Februar ist immer kalt und wolkig. Ich verstehe es nicht!'

'Es ist der Klimawandel', sagt Ivan. In der Schule lernt Ivan etwas über Umweltverschmutzung und Müll. Das Wetter ändert sich aufgrund von Veränderungen in der Atmosphäre . Der Klimawandel ist der Unterschied im Wetter im Laufe der Zeit.

'Ich weiß nichts über den Klimawandel', sagt Opa. 'Ich sage das Wetter nach dem, was ich voraus sehe.'

'Was meinst du damit?' fragte Ivan.

'Heute Morgen ist der Himmel rot', sagt Opa, 'daher weiß ich, dass ein

Sturm kommt.'Wie?' fragte Ivan.

'Roter Himmel am Morgen, Seeleute sind gewarnt, roter Himmel in der Nacht, Seemannsfreude', Opa erzählt Ivan von diesem Sprichwort.

Wenn der Himmel bei Sonnenaufgang rot ist, bedeutet das, dass Wasser in der Luft ist. Das Licht der Sonne leuchtet rot. Der Sturm kommt auf dich zu. Wenn der Himmel bei Sonnenuntergang rot ist, geht das schlechte Wetter. Ohne Wetterexperten beobachten die Menschen den Himmel nach Hinweisen über das Wetter.

'Wie sagen Wetterexperten das Wetter voraus?', fragt Ivan.

'Sie schauen sich Muster in der Atmosphäre an', sagt Oma. 'Sie schauen auf die Temperatur, ob es heiß oder kalt ist. Und sie schauen auf den Luftdruck, was in der Atmosphäre passiert.'

'Ich prognostiziere das Wetter anders', sagt Opa. 'Ich weiß zum Beispiel, dass es heute regnen wird.'

'Wie?'fragt Ivan.

'Die Katze', sagt Opa. Ivan sieht die Katze an. Die Katze öffnet den Mund und sagt HATSCHI.

'Wenn die Katze niest oder schnarcht, bedeutet das, dass Regen kommt', sagt Opa. 'Es mag nieseln oder es mag sehr regnerisch sein, aber es wird regnen.'

Plötzlich hören sie ein lautes Geräusch. Ivan schaut aus dem Fenster. Regentropfen fallen schwer, der Regen ist laut. Ivan kann nicht hören, was sein Großvater sagt.

'Was?' sagt Ivan.

'Es regnet in Strömen', sagt Opa, lächelnd.

'Ha!' lacht Ivan.

'Ich kenne einen anderen Weg, das Wetter zu sagen', sagt Oma.

Oma beobachtet die Spinnen, um zu sehen, wann das Wetter kalt sein wird. Am Ende des Sommers ändert sich das Wetter. Der Herbst bringt frische, kühle Luft. Oma weiß, wenn Spinnen hereinkommen, bedeutet das, dass kaltes Wetter kommt. Spinnen machen es sich vor dem Winter drinnen gemütlich. So weiß Oma, wann das Winterwetter kommt.

Der Regen hört auf, Großvater und Ivan gehen raus. Opa und Oma leben in einem Haus im Wald. Das Haus hat Bäume um sich herum, es ist ein kleines Haus. Ivan ist kalt in seinem T-Shirt. Das Wetter ist nicht sonnig. Die Luft bewegt sich, es ist windig . Der Wind bläst durch Ivans Haar.

'Jetzt ist es kalt ', sagt Ivan.

'Ja', sagt Opa. 'Wie hoch ist die Temperatur?'

'Keine Ahnung', sagt Ivan. 'Ich habe kein Thermometer.'

'Du brauchst keins', sagt Opa. Großvater sagt Ivan, er soll zuhören. Ivan hört ein Geräusch: Kri-Kri-Kri-Kri. Es ist ein Insekt. Das Kri-Kri-Kri ist der Klang von Grillen, erklärt Großvater Ivan. Ivan zählt das Kri für 14 Sekunden. Großvater fügt 40 zu dieser Zahl hinzu. Das ist die Temperatur draußen. Ivan wusste nicht, Grillen sind wie Thermometer.

Oma kommt aus dem Haus. Sie lächelt, sie sieht Ivan beim Zählen des Grillengeräusches zu. 'Zeit für Kekse und Milch!'sagt sie.

'Hurra!'sagt Ivan.

'Oh, schau!'sagt Oma. 'Es ist ein Regenbogen.'Der Regenbogen geht vom Haus bis zum Wald. Er hat viele Farben: rot, orange, gelb, blau und grün. Der Regenbogen ist wunderschön, Oma, Opa und Ivan schauen sich den Regenbogen an. Er verschwindet und sie gehen hinein.

'Kekse und Milch für alle', sagt Oma. Sie gibt Ivan einen warmen Schokoladenkeks.

'Nicht für mich', sagt Opa. 'Ich will Tee.'

'Warum Tee?'sagt Oma. Sie hält zwei Gläser mit Milch in den Händen.

'Ich fühle mich nicht wohl ', sagt Opa. Er lacht, Ivan und Oma lachen mit ihm.

ÜBERSETZUNG/ TRANSLATION

Ivan is twelve years old. He visits his grandparents on weekends. He loves to visit his grandparents. Grandma gives him cookies and milk every day. Grandpa teaches him great things. This weekend he is going to see them.

It is February. Where Ivan is, it is winter. It usually snows in February. Ivan loves the snow. He plays in it and rolls it into balls. This February weekend, the weather is different. The sun is shining; it is sunny and almost hot! Ivan wears a T-shirt to his grandparents' house.

'Hi, grandpa! Hi, grandma!'says Ivan. 'Hi, Ivan!' says grandma.

'Ivan! How are you?' asks grandpa.

'I'm fine,' he says and hugs his grandparents. Ivan says goodbye to his mother.

They go into the house. 'This weather is strange,' says Grandma. 'February is always cold and cloudy. I don't understand it!'

'It's climate change,' Ivan says. At school, Ivan learns about pollution and garbage. The weather changes because of changes in the atmosphere . Climate change is the difference in weather over time.

'I don't know anything about climate change,' says Grandpa. 'I tell the weather by what I see ahead.'

'What do you mean by that?' asked Ivan.

'This morning the sky is red,' said Grandpa, 'that's how I know a Storm is coming.'How?' asked Ivan.

'Red sky in the morning, sailors are warned, red sky at night, sailor's delight,' Grandpa tells Ivan about this proverb.

'If the sky is red at sunrise, it means there is water in the air. The light of the sun shines red. The storm is coming your way. If the sky is red at sunset, the bad weather is going. Without weather experts, people watch the sky for clues about the weather.

'How do weather experts predict the weather?' asks Ivan.

'They look at patterns in the atmosphere,' says Grandma. 'They look at the temperature, whether it's hot or cold. And they look at air pressure, what's happening in the atmosphere.'

'I forecast the weather differently,' Grandpa says. 'For example, I know it's going to rain today.'

'How?'asks Ivan.

'The cat,' says Grandpa. Ivan looks at the cat. The cat opens its mouth and says HATSCHI.

'If the cat sneezes or snores, it means rain is coming,' says Grandpa. 'It may drizzle or it may be very rainy, but it will rain.'

Suddenly they hear a loud noise. Ivan looks out of the window. Raindrops are falling heavily, the rain is loud. Ivan can't hear what his grandfather is saying.

'What?' says Ivan.

'It's pouring,' says Grandpa, smiling.

'Haha!' laughs Ivan.

'I know another way to tell the weather,' says Grandma.

Grandma watches the spiders to see when the weather will be cold. At the end of summer, the weather changes. Autumn brings fresh, cool air. Grandma knows when spiders come in, it means cold weather is coming. Spiders make themselves comfortable inside before winter. So grandma knows when winter weather is coming.

The rain stops, Grandpa and Ivan go outside. Grandpa and Grandma live in a house in the forest. The house has trees around it, it is a small house. Ivan is cold in his T-shirt. The weather is not sunny. The air is moving, it is windy . The wind blows through Ivan's hair.

'It's cold now ', Ivan says.

'Yes,' says grandpa. 'What's the temperature?'

'I don't know,' says Ivan. 'I don't have a thermometer.'

'You don't need one,' says Grandpa. Grandpa tells Ivan to listen. Ivan hears a sound: kri-kri-kri. It is an insect. The kri-kri-kri is the sound of crickets, Grandpa explains to Ivan. Ivan counts the kri for 14 seconds. Grandfather adds 40 to that number. That's the temperature outside. Ivan didn't know, crickets are like thermometers.

Grandma comes out of the house. She smiles, watching Ivan count the cricket sound. 'Time for cookies and milk!'she says.

'Hooray!'says Ivan.

'Oh, look!'says Grandma. 'It's a rainbow.'The rainbow goes from the house to the forest. It has many colors: red, orange, yellow, blue and green. The rainbow is beautiful. Grandma, Grandpa and Ivan look at the rainbow. He disappears and they go inside.

'Cookies and milk for everyone,' Grandma says. She gives Ivan a warm chocolate cookie.

'Not for me,' says Grandpa. 'I want tea.'

'Why tea?'says Grandma. She holds two glasses with milk in her hands.

'I don't feel well,' says Grandpa. He laughs, Ivan and Grandma laugh with him.

ZUSAMMENFASSUNG/ SUMMARY

Ivan is twelve years old and visits his grandparents on weekends. This February weekend, the weather is different and Ivan wears a T-shirt to his grandparents' house. Grandpa teaches him about climate change, which is the difference in weather over time. He also tells Ivan about the proverb 'Red sky in the morning, sailors are warned, red sky at night, sailor's delight' which states that if the sky is red at sunrise, there is water in the air and the storm is coming. Weather experts predict the weather by looking at patterns in the atmosphere, but Grandma and Grandpa forecast the weather differently.

Grandma watches the spiders to see when the weather will be cold, while Grandpa watches the cat to predict rain. When the rain stops, Grandpa and Ivan go outside. Grandpa and Grandma live in a small house in the forest. It is cold and windy, and Grandpa tells Ivan to listen for the sound of crickets. Ivan counts the kri-kri sound for 14 seconds and Grandpa adds 40 to that number, which is the temperature outside.

Grandma comes out of the house with cookies and milk for everyone, but Grandpa wants tea. He laughs, Ivan and Grandma laugh with him.

WORTSCHATZ!

Winter schneien	winter to snow
Wetter	weather
sonnig	sunny
heiß	hot
kalt	cold
wolkig	cloudy
Klimawandel	climate change
Atmosphäre	atmosphere
voraussagen	predict
Himmel	sky
Sturm	storm
Temperatur	temperature
In Strömen regnen	raining cats and dogs
Sommer	summer
Wetterexperten	weathermen

Herbst	autumn
windig	windy
nieseln	drizzle

FRAGEN

Wählen Sie nur eine Antwort pro Frage aus.

1. Wie ist das Wetter im Februar normalerweise?

a) heiß

b) kalt

c) sonnig

d) frisch

2. Woher weiß Opa, wie das Wetter sein wird?

a) er sieht Fernsehen

b) Wetterexperten

c) er beobachtet die Natur

d) er sagt das Wetter voraus

3. Was bedeutet es, wenn es in Strömen regnet? ?

a) es regnet Ströme

b) es regnet nur ein wenig

c) Flüsse fließen schneller

d) es regnet sehr stark

4. Was bedeutet es, wenn Spinnen reinkommen?

a) sie sind hungrig

b) sie sind bereit, Eier zu legen

c) Kälte kommt auf uns zu

d) warmes Wetter kommt

5. Warum bittet Opa um Tee statt Milch?

a) er fühlt sich etwas krank

b) er ist allergisch gegen Milch

c) er will ein heißes Getränk

d) um Oma wütend zu machen

ANTWORTEN

1. Wie ist das Wetter im Februar normalerweise?

b) kalt

2. Woher weiß Opa, wie das Wetter sein wird?

d) er sagt das Wetter voraus

3. Was bedeutet es, wenn es in Strömen regnet?

d) es regnet sehr stark

4. Was bedeutet es, wenn Spinnen reinkommen?

c) Kälte kommt auf uns zu

5. Warum bittet Opa um Tee statt Milch?

a) er fühlt sich etwas krank

ANTWORTEN/ ANSWERS

1. How is the weather usually in february?

b) cold

2) How does Grandpa know what the weather will be like?

d) he predicts the weather

3. what does it mean to rain in torrents?

d) it is raining very hard

4. what does it mean when spiders come in?

c) cold is coming

5. Why does grandpa ask for tea instead of milk?

a) he feels a little sick

KAPITEL 4

Weniges, aber das Wenige recht. Das ist der
Grundsatz allen echten Unterrichts
von Heinrich Wilhelm Josias Thiersch

DER POLIZIST

HANDLUNG

Toms Vater ist Polizist. Er beschützt die Bürger und passt auf, dass nichts passiert. 'Es ist nicht leicht, Polizist zu sein', sagt er immer. Manchmal arbeitet Toms Vater morgens, manchmal mittags und manchmal abends. Es nennt sich Schichtdienst. Die Kollegen von Toms Vater, kommen oft zu Besuch. Manchmal kommen sie mit dem Polizeiauto. Tom freut sich jedes Mal sehr. Er findet Polizeiautos interessant. In der Zukunft will Tom auch Polizist werden.

'Ich will auch Bürger beschützen und aufpassen, dass nichts passiert', sagt Tom oft zu seinem Vater. Sein Vater lacht. 'Das ist gut. Polizist ist ein wichtiger Beruf.', sagt er. Tom denkt das auch. In seiner Freizeit liest Tom Bücher über Polizisten. Er muss wissen, was gute Polizisten machen, sagt er. Sein Vater sagt, dass das eine gute Idee ist.

Wenn Tom mit einem Buch fertig ist, dann kauft sein Vater ein neues Buch. Tom hat sehr viele Bücher über Polizisten, aber er will mehr. Er liest jeden Monat zwei (2) Bücher.

ÜBERSETZUNG/ TRANSLATION/ SUMMARY

Tom's father is a policeman. He protects the citizens and makes sure that nothing happens. 'It's not easy being a policeman,' he always says. Sometimes Tom's father works in the morning, sometimes at noon and sometimes in the evening.

He calls it shift work. The colleagues, from Tom's father, often come to visit. Sometimes they come with the police car. Tom is very happy every time. He finds police cars interesting. In the future Tom also wants to become a policeman.

'I also want to protect citizens and make sure nothing happens,' Tom often tells his father.

His father laughs. 'That's good. A policeman is an important job,' he says. Tom thinks so, too. In his spare time, Tom reads books about policemen. He needs to know what good cops do, he says. His father says that's a good idea.

When Tom finishes a book, his father buys a new book. Tom has a lot of books about policemen, but he wants more. He reads two 2 books every month.

WORTSCHATZ

Polizist	Policeman
beschützt	protects
Bürger	citizen
aufpassen	watch
Beruf	profession
fertig	ready
lauft	run
Freizeit	free time

denkt	thinks

FRAGEN

Wählen Sie nur eine Antwort pro Frage aus.

1. Was macht Toms Vater?
a) Polizist
b) Artz
c) Journalist
d) Maler

2. Was ist Schichtdienst?
a) Alltägliche arbeit
b) jeden Tag zu verschiedenen Zeiten zu arbeiten
c) Arbeiten nach unserer Wahl
d) Arbeitslosigkeit

3. Wer kommt oft zu Besuch?
a) Toms Kollegen
b) Nachbarn
c) Freunde
d) Oma und Opa

4. Was will Tom in Zukunft werden? Was macht ein Polizist?

5. Wie viele Bücher liest Tom jeden Monat?
a) Drei
b) Vier
c) Elf
d) Zwei

ANTWORTEN

1. Was macht Toms Vater?

a) Polizist

2. Was ist Schichtdienst?

b) jeden Tag zu verschiedenen Zeiten zu arbeiten

3. Wer kommt oft zu Besuch?

a) Toms Kollegen

4. Was will Tom in Zukunft werden? Was macht ein Polizist?

5. Wie viele Bücher liest Tom jeden Monat?

d) Zwei

ENGLISCH

1. What does Tom's father do?

a) Police officer

2. What is shift work?

b) working at different times every day

3. Who often comes to visit?

a) Tom's colleagues

4. What does Tom want to be in the future? What does a police officer do?

5. How many books does Tom read each month?

d) Two

KAPITEL 5

'Das Ziel der Wünsche steht niemals still.'
von George Gerhard Reisenberg

DAS WESEN; DER AUSFLUG

TEIL 1

Silvia ist eine Frau, die gern wandert. Jedes Wochenende nahm sie ihren Rucksack, ihre Wasserflasche, ihre Bergkleidung und lief bis zum Berg Wolfskopf. Das ist ein Berg in Niedersachsen, im Norden Deutschlands.

Am ersten Samstag im Monat verabredete sie sich mit ihrem Freund Jochen. Da Jochen ebenfalls gern wanderte, begleitete er Silvia bei ihrem Ausflug. Sie sahen sich am Anfang des Weges und begrüßten sich:

'Silvia! Hier bin ich!', rief Jochen.
'Ich sehe dich! Ich komme!'

Silvia hielt an und wartete auf Jochen. Jochen rannte schnell zu Silvia. 'Jochen, renne nicht so.' Sonst bist du schnell erschöpft.'
'Keine Sorge, ich habe ein Energie-Getränk für den Weg.'

Der Wolfskopf ist ein bekannter Berg in Niedersachsen, wohin viele Bergsteiger zum Wandern oder Spazieren gehen. Einige Familien fahren dort mit dem Auto zum Abendessen hin, andere Leute, um professionelle Fotos zu machen oder im Sommer zu zelten.

Niedersachsen ist eine Region Deutschlands mit sehr milden Temperaturen. In Niedersachsen regnet es normalerweise viel, es ist neblig und der Sommer ist nicht sehr heiß. Es sind mittlere Temperaturen. Silvia und Jochen nutzen das Juliwetter aus, wenn es warm ist und sie keine Jacke brauchen.

'Jochen, welchen Weg nehmen wir? Den rechten oder den linken? 'Ich bevorzuge den linken Weg.'
'Aber ich bevorzuge den rechten Weg.'
Warum, Silvia?'
Über diesen Weg gibt es eine Legende. Man sagt, dass oft ein großes
behaartes Wesen gesehen wurde. 'Glaubst du diese Geschichten?' Wir könnten da lang gehen. 'Na gut, Silvia.
Gehen wir.'

Eine Stunde später gingen sie auf einem schmalen Weg, der von Bäumen umgeben war, so dass man kaum noch die Sonne am Himmel sah.
Silvia fragte Jochen:
'Glaubst du, dass es ungewöhnliche Wesen in den Wäldern gibt?'
'Ich glaube nicht.'
'Warum?'
'Ich habe niemals so ein Wesen gesehen. Hast du?'
'Nicht in diesem Wald.'

Jochen fragte sich, was sie damit meinte, aber er fragte sie lieber nicht und ging weiter.
Einige Kilometer später liefen die beiden Freunde an Bäumen und Wegen vorbei. Man sah die Sonne nicht, und ihre Schritte führten zu einem See, an dem ein Haus stand. Das Haus war aus Holz und schien alt zu sein.

'Guck mal da, Jochen.'
'Wo?'
'Da! Da ist ein Holzhaus.'
'Ah, ja! Ich sehe es! Gehen wir?'
'Und wenn da jemand ist?'
'Hab keine Angst, Jochen. Da ist sicher niemand.'

Das Pärchen ging bis zum Haus und erforschte den Ort, bevor sie hineingingen.

Silvia sagte:

'Das Haus scheint vor langer Zeit gebaut worden zu sein.'

'Ja, Silvia. Sieh dir mal den Zustand der Fenster und des Holzes an. Sie sind sehr alt. Komm her!'

Sie näherten sich dem Seeufer, wo kleine Wellen ein kleines Boot bewegten. Das Boot sah genau so alt aus wie das Haus.

'Silvia, steigen wir ein?'

'Wozu?'

Wir können zur Mitte des Sees fahren. Lass uns Spaß haben! Komm!'

Silvia und Jochen stiegen in das Boot und stellten ihre Rucksäcke ab. Das Holz sah alt und kaputt aus. Es gab zwei Ruder. Sie benutzten die Ruder, um in die Mitte des Sees zu kommen.

Silvia sagte zu Jochen:

'Wie gut man es hier hat, Jochen!'

'Ja, das stimmt. Obwohl es viele Bäume gibt, können wir die Sonne von hier aus perfekt sehen.'

'Ja. Möchtest du etwas essen?'

'Klar, Silvia! Was hast du mitgebracht?'

Silvia nahm Kuchen, Energie-Getränke und Butterbrote aus ihrem Rucksack.

'Was möchtest du?'

'Das Butterbrot sieht lecker aus.'

'Ich möchte es nicht, also ist es für dich, Jochen.'Danke!'

Sie aßen in Ruhe, während sich das Boot in der Mitte des Sees hielt. Plötzlich hörten sie ein Geräusch, das von dem Haus kam:

'Hast du das gehört?', sagte Jochen zu Silvia.

'Ja, das habe ich', antwortete sie mit erschrockenem Gesicht. 'Ich glaube, es kommt aus dem Haus.'

'Das glaube ich auch. Komm!'

Jochen und Silvia ruderten ohne Pause bis sie ans Ufer kamen. Sie setzten sich wieder ihre Rucksäcke auf und gingen bis zum alten Holzhaus.

'Jochen, ich habe dir vorher nichts gesagt, aber ich wollte zu diesem Haus gehen.'

'Warum? Ich habe angenommen, dass wir wandern gehen.'

'Ja, aber in den Wäldern gibt es viele verlassene Hütten und ich

erforsche gerne.'

'Dann gehen wir doch in das Haus.'

Einige Schritte später öffneten sie die Haustür, und das Pärchen ging hinein. Drinnen war alles sehr schmutzig

und verlassen. Das Haus schien seit vielen Jahren nicht mehr benutzt worden zu sein. Jetzt gab es nichts als Staub.

'Silvia, schau das mal an!'

'Was?'

'Hier, neben dem Fenster.'

Silvia schaute. Auf dem Boden waren sehr große Abdrücke im Staub. 'Was glaubst du, wovon die Abdrücke sein

können?'

'Ich glaube, sie sind von einem Bär', sagte Silvia.

'Von einem Bär, Silvia? Es gibt keine Bären in der Nähe! Die Bären

sind auf einem anderen Berg, viele Kilometer weit weg.'

'Dann weiß ich nicht, von wem sie sein können. Lass uns verschwinden!'

Ohne Vorwarnung wurden sie von Lärm in der Küche überrascht, und sie konnten eine große, haarige Figur aus der Tür laufen sehen, die alles kaputt machte. Das Wesen grunzte und lief sehr schnell. Das Pärchen war wie gelähmt, bis sie das Wesen aus den Augen verloren.

ÜBERSETZUNG/ TRANSLATION

Silvia is a woman who loves to hike. Every weekend she took her backpack, her water bottle, her mountain clothes and walked up to the mountain Wolfskopf. This is a mountain in Lower Saxony, in the north of Germany.

On the first Saturday of the month, she arranged to meet her boyfriend Jochen. Since Jochen also liked to hike, he accompanied Silvia on her outing. They saw each other at the beginning of the trail and greeted each other:

Silvia! Here I am!' exclaimed Jochen.

'I see you! I'm coming!'

Silvia stopped and waited for Jochen. Jochen quickly ran to Silvia. 'Jochen, don't run like that. Otherwise you'll be exhausted quickly.'

'Don't worry, I have an energy drink for the road.'

Wolfskopf is a famous mountain in Lower Saxony, where many climbers go to hike or run. Some families go there by car for dinner, other people take professional photos or to camp in summer.

Lower Saxony is a region of Germany with very mild temperatures. In Lower Saxony it usually rains a lot, it is foggy and the summer is not very hot. It is medium temperature. Silvia and Jochen take advantage of the July weather when it is warm and they don't need a jacket.

'Jochen, which way do we take? The right way or the left way?' 'I prefer the left way.'

'But I prefer the right way.'

Why, Silvia?'

'There is a legend about this path. They say that often a great hairy creature

'Do you believe those stories?' 'We could go that way.' 'All right, Silvia. Let's go.'

An hour later, they were walking along a narrow path surrounded by trees, so that you could hardly see the sun in the sky.

Silvia asked Jochen:

'Do you think there are unusual creatures in the woods?'

'I don't think so.'

'Why?

'I have never seen a creature. Have you?'

'Not in this forest.'

Jochen wondered what she meant by that, but he preferred not to ask her and kept walking.

A few miles later, the two friends walked past trees and paths. The sun could not be seen, and their steps led to a lake where a house stood. The house was made of wood and seemed old.

'Look there, Jochen.'

'Where?

'There, there's a wooden house.'

'Ah, yes! I see it! Shall we go?'

'What if there's someone there?'

'Don't be afraid, Jochen. I'm sure there's no one there.'

The couple walked up to the house and explored the place before going inside.

Silvia said:

'The house seems to have been built a long time ago.'

'Yes, Silvia. Look at the condition of the windows and the wood. They are very old. Come here.'

They approached the lake shore where small waves were moving a small boat. The boat looked just as old as the house.

'Silvia, shall we get in?

'What for?

'We can go to the middle of the lake. Let's have fun!' 'Come on!'

Silvia and Jochen got into the boat and put down their backpacks. The wood looked old and broken. There were two oars. They used the oars to get to the middle of the lake.

Silvia said to Jochen:

'How good you have it here, Jochen!'

'Yes, it is. Although there are many trees, we can see the sun perfectly from here.'

'Yes. Would you like something to eat?'

'Sure, Silvia! What did you bring?'

Silvia took cakes, energy drinks and sandwiches from her backpack.

'What do you want?

'The sandwich looks delicious.'

'I don't want it, so it's for you, Jochen.'Thanks!'

They ate in silence while the boat kept in the middle of the lake. Suddenly they heard a noise coming from the house:

'Did you hear that?' said Jochen to Silvia.

'Yes, I did,' she answered with a startled face. 'I think it's coming from the house.'

'I think so, too. Come!'

Jochen and Silvia rowed without pause until they reached the shore. They put on their backpacks again and walked up to the old wooden house.

'Jochen, I didn't tell you before, but I wanted to go to this house.'

'Why?' I assumed we were going hiking.'

'Yes, but there are many abandoned cabins in the woods and I like to explore.'

'Then let's go into the house.'

A few steps later they opened the front door and the couple went inside. Inside, everything was very dirty and abandoned. The house seemed not to have been used for many years. Now there was nothing but dust.

'Silvia, look at this!

'What?

'Here, next to the window.'

Silvia looked. There were very big prints in the dust on the floor. 'What do you think the prints could be from?'

'I think they are from a bear,' said Silvia.

'From a bear, Silvia? There are no bears around! The bears are on another mountain, many miles away.'

'Then I don't know who they can be from. Let's get out of here!'

Without warning, they were surprised by noise in the kitchen, and they could see a large, hairy figure running out of the door, breaking everything. The creature grunted and ran very fast. The couple was paralyzed until they lost sight of the creature.

ZUSAMMENFASSUNG/ SUMMARY

Silvia is a woman who loves to hike and meets her boyfriend Jochen on the first Saturday of the month. They hike up to Wolfskopf, a famous mountain in Lower Saxony, where many climbers go to hike or run. Silvia and Jochen take advantage of the July weather when it is warm and they don't need a jacket. An hour later, they are walking along a narrow path surrounded by trees and the sun is not visible. Silvia asks Jochen if he has ever seen a creature in the woods, but he prefers not to ask her and keeps walking.

The couple explored a house built a long time ago and saw a small boat on the lake shore. Silvia and Jochen got into the boat and used the oars to get to the middle of the lake. Silvia brought cakes, energy drinks and sandwiches, and they ate in silence until they heard a noise coming from the house. Jochen and Silvia rowed to an old wooden house and decided to explore it. Inside, everything was dirty and abandoned, and Silvia noticed large prints in the dust on the floor.

Suddenly, they were surprised by noise in the kitchen and saw a large, hairy figure running out of the door. The couple was paralyzed until they lost sight of the creature.

WORTSCHATZ

das Wesen	creature
wandern	to hike
bekannt	well-known, popular
die Freizeitaktivität	leisure acitivy
beliebt	popular
der Ausflug	excursion
sich auf den Weg machen	set off
Sonst geht uns gleich die Puste aus.	'Otherwise we might run out of steam soon.'
das Energiegetränk	energy drink
Behaart	Furry, hairy
wie gelähmt	as though they were paralyzed
inzwischen	in the meantime
grunzen	grunt

plötzlich	all of the sudden, suddenly
dicht	dense
verlassen seltsam	abandoned strange
das Geräusch	noise
der Abdruck	footprint
der Staub	dust
der Schritt	step
die Hütte	hut/ cottage
das Holz	wood
der Steg	boat landing, dock
das Butterbrot	sandwich
das Ruder	oar

FRAGEN

Wählen Sie nur eine Antwort pro Frage aus.

1. Silvia und Jochen sind aus:

a. Köln

b. Niedersachsen

c. Düsseldorf

d. Bayern

2. Der Ausflug geht zu:

a. Einem Berg

b. Einem Strand

c. Einem kleinen Dorf

d. Einer Stadt

3. Auf einem Weg gehend finden sie:

a. Ein Dorf

b. Eine Stadt

c. Ein Geschäft

d. Ein Haus

4. Als sie das Boot sehen:

a. Setzen sie sich hinein

b. Schlafen sie auf ihm

c. Nutzen sie es, um sich zu wärmen

d. Nutzen sie es, um zur Mitte des Sees zu fahren

5. Am Ende des Kapitels hören sie Lärm:

a. Auf dem Boot

b. In der Küche

c. Im Saal

d. Im Wald

ANTWORTEN

1. Silvia und Jochen sind aus:

b. Niedersachsen

2. Der Ausflug geht zu:

a. Einem Berg

3. Auf einem Weg gehend finden sie:

d. Ein Haus

4. Als sie das Boot sehen:

d. Nutzen sie es, um zur Mitte des Sees zu fahren

5. Am Ende des Kapitels hören sie Lärm:

b. In der Küche

ENGLISCH

1. Silvia and Jochen are out:

b. Lower Saxony

2. the trip goes to:

a. A mountain

3. walking on a path they find:

d. A house

4. when they see the boat

d. Use it to go to the middle of the lake

5. At the end of the chapter, they hear noise:

b. In the kitchen

TEIL 2/PART 2!

'Hast du das gesehen, Silvia?'

'Ja! Was war das?'

'Keine Ahnung! Aber es war ein großes und hässliches Wesen.' 'Was machen wir jetzt, Jochen?'

'Lass uns hinterhergehen.'

'Was? Du willst es verfolgen?'

'Natürlich!'

Jochen und Silvia gingen aus dem alten Holzhaus. Sie folgten den Abdrücken bis in den Wald.

'Hier sind viele Bäume und viele Wege', sagte Jochen. 'Wir müssen uns trennen.'

'Bist du verrückt, Jochen! Uns trennen? Da läuft ein großes und hässliches Wesen frei herum, und wir wissen nicht, was es ist!'

'Ja schon, Silvia. Aber falls wir das Wesen mit dem Handy filmen können, kommen wir vielleicht in die Nachrichten.'

'Ist doch egal!'

'Ich würde gerne in die Nachrichten kommen.'

Nach zwei Stunden gingen Silvia und Jochen immer noch durch den Wald. Sie suchten das Wesen. Silvia glaubte nicht mehr, dass das Wesen echt sein könnte. Vielleicht war das alles nur ein schlechter Traum?

Jochen aber sagte immer wieder, dass das Wesen bestimmt echt sei. Ein Tier wie ein Yeti, das noch nie gefilmt wurde.

Die beiden kamen an eine besonders dichte Stelle im Wald. Jochen sagte Silvia, sie solle warten. Vielleicht versteckte sich das Wesen hier? Er lächelte Silvia an und verschwand zwischen den Bäumen.

Jochen kam nicht wieder heraus. Silvia wartete einige Minuten. Sie hörte nichts, sie sah nichts. Nach einer Stunde immer noch kein Jochen!

Silvia schaute auf ihr Handy. Sie hatte an dieser Stelle keinen Empfang. Niemand konnte ihr helfen. Da es schon sehr spät war und sie fast nichts mehr sehen konnte, ging sie zum Haus zurück. Sie setzte sich auf ein altes Bett, das dort stand und wartete auf Jochen. Sie holte ein Butterbrot aus ihrem Rucksack und aß. Am Ende schlief sie ein.

Sehr früh am nächsten Morgen wachte Silvia auf. Immer noch kein Jochen! Silvia machte sich große Sorgen um Jochen. Sie musste jetzt Hilfe holen. Stundenlang ging sie den Weg zurück. Schließlich kam sie in ein Dorf.

Im Dorf war viel los. Die Leute arbeiteten in ihren Gärten. Kinder rannten und spielten auf dem Weg zur Schule, Autos fuhren vorbei. Es roch nach Frühstück. Silvia hatte Lust auf einen Kaffee und ging ins Dorfcafé. Dort frühstückten viele Leute. Silvia hatte immer noch keinen Empfang auf ihrem Handy.

Sie ging zum Kellner und sagte:

'Guten Tag.'

'Guten Tag. Was wünschen Sie?'

'Darf ich das Telefon benutzen?' 'Natürlich, gerne. Es ist dort an der Wand.' 'Danke.'

'Wünschen Sie noch etwas?' 'Ja, bitte einen Kaffee.'

Silvia ging zum Telefon und wählte Jochens Nummer. Vielleicht war ihr Handy das Problem. Aber nein. Sein Telefon hatte auch keinen Empfang. Sie dachte nach und entschied: ‚Ich rufe bei Jochen zu Hause an.‘

Das Telefon klingelte einmal, zweimal, dreimal. Warum nahm niemand ab? Was war bloß los? Jochen wohnte bei seinem Bruder. Der war normalerweise den ganzen Tag zu Hause, weil er dort arbeitete. Silvia trank ihren Kaffee und rief noch einmal an. Niemand nahm ab.

Silvia verließ das Café und setzte sich auf eine Bank. Dort dachte sie noch einmal nach. Silvia war eine sehr intelligente Frau, die selten nervös wurde.

Sie beschloss, direkt zu Jochens Haus zu fahren. Vielleicht war er ja da und schlief? Auf der Straße stand ein Taxi. Der Fahrer öffnete die Tür und Silvia stieg ein.

'Sind Sie auf dem Weg zur Arbeit?', fragte der Taxifahrer nach einer Weile.

'Nein, ich möchte einen Freund zu Hause besuchen.'

'Was für ein Glück! Ich muss den ganzen Tag arbeiten!'

Silvia sagte nichts mehr. Der Taxifahrer war sehr nett, aber sie hatte keine Lust zu reden. Sie wollte nur noch Jochen finden. Sie glaubte nicht, dass es ein seltsames Wesen im Wald gab. Sie wollte endlich wissen, wo ihr Freund war.

'Da sind wir', sagte der Taxifahrer zu Silvia. 'Das macht dann 9,50 Euro.'

'Hier bitte, der Rest ist für Sie.' 'Danke! Schönen Tag noch!' 'Warten Sie bitte einen Moment?' 'Ja, kein Problem.'

Silvia stieg aus und ging zu Jochens Haus. Es war ein großes Haus mit zwei Etagen, einem Garten und einer Garage. Es befand sich in einem sehr schönen und ruhigen Viertel. Es gab auch Geschäfte, wo man Obst, Brot und alles Notwendige kaufen konnte. Jochens Auto stand vor dem Haus. War Jochen doch schon zu Hause? Hatte er vielleicht seinen Bruder angerufen?

Silvia war ratlos. Wenn Jochen mit dem Auto nach Hause gefahren war, warum hatte sie dann keine Nachricht auf ihrem Handy?

Silvia klingelte dreimal an der Tür, aber niemand antwortete.

Sie ging besorgt zum Haus ihrer beiden Freundinnen Claudia und Veronika. Aber die beiden waren auch nicht zu Hause. Und ihre Handys waren ausgeschaltet. Was war nur los? Seitdem sie dieses Monster getroffen hatten, waren alle ihre Freunde verschwunden.

Etwas musste passieren. Die Polizei konnte sie nicht anrufen. Sie konnte doch der Polizei nichts einem haarigen Wesen im Wald erzählen. Außerdem stand Jochens Auto vor der Tür. Aber wo war er? War er doch verletzt oder krank und lag im Krankenhaus? Sie musste selbst die Initiative ergreifen und ihn finden.

Wenige Minuten später stieg sie wieder ins Taxi. Diesmal fand sie einen kürzeren Weg zum Haus am See. Als sie aus dem Wald kam, war sie für einen Moment wie gelähmt: In der dunklen Hütte war Licht. Und Silvia wusste genau, dass sie am Morgen das Licht ausgemacht hatte.

ÜBERSETZUNG/ TRANSLATION

'Did you see that, Silvia?'

'Yes! What was that?'

'I don't know! But it was a big and ugly creature.' 'What are we going to do, Jochen?'

'Let's go after it.'

'What, you want to go after it?'

'Of course!'

Jochen and Silvia walked out of the old wooden house. They followed the prints into the forest.

'There are a lot of trees here and a lot of trails,' Jochen said. 'We'll have to split up.'

'Are you crazy, Jochen! Separate us? There's a big and ugly creature on the loose, and we don't know what it is!'

'Yes, we do, Silvia. But if we can film the creature with our cell phones, we might make the news.'

'Who cares!'

'I'd love to get on the news.'

After two hours, Silvia and Jochen were still walking through the forest. They were looking for the creature. Silvia no longer believed the creature could be real. Maybe it was all just a bad dream?

Jochen, however, kept saying that the creature was definitely real. An animal like a Yeti that had never been filmed before.

The two came to a particularly dense spot in the forest. Jochen told Silvia to wait. Maybe the creature was hiding here? He smiled at Silvia and disappeared between the trees.

Jochen did not come out again. Silvia waited a few minutes. She heard nothing, she saw nothing. After an hour still no Jochen!

Silvia looked at her cell phone. She had no reception at this point. Nobody could help her. Since it was already very late and she could see almost nothing, she went back to the house. She sat down on an old bed that was there and waited for Jochen. She took a sandwich out of her backpack and ate. In the end, she fell asleep.

Very early the next morning Silvia woke up. Still no Jochen! Silvia was very worried about Jochen. She had to get help now. For hours she walked back the way she came. Finally she came to a village.

There was a lot going on in the village. People were working in their gardens. Children ran and played on the way to school, cars drove by. It smelled like breakfast. Silvia felt like having a coffee and went to the village café. Many people were having breakfast there. Silvia still had no reception on her cell phone. She went to the waiter and said:

'Good afternoon.'

'Good afternoon. What do you want?'

'May I use the phone?' 'Of course, you're welcome to. It's there on the wall.' 'Thank you.'

'Would you like anything else?' 'Yes, a coffee, please.'

Silvia went to the phone and dialed Jochen's number. Maybe her cell phone was the problem. But no. His phone had no reception either. She thought and decided, 'I'll call Jochen's house.'

The phone rang once, twice, three times. Why didn't anyone pick up? What was going on? Jochen lived with his brother. He was usually at home all day because he worked there.

Silvia drank her coffee and called again. No one answered.

Silvia left the café and sat down on a bench. There she thought again. Silvia was a very intelligent woman who rarely got nervous.

She decided to go directly to Jochen's house. Maybe he was there and asleep? There was a cab on the street. The driver opened the door and Silvia got in.

'Are you on your way to work?' the cab driver asked after a while.

'No, I want to visit a friend at home.'

'What luck! I have to work all day!'

Silvia said no more. The cab driver was very nice, but she didn't feel like talking. She just wanted to find Jochen. She didn't believe there was a strange creature in the forest. She finally wanted to know where her friend was.

'Here we are,' the cab driver said to Silvia. 'That will be 9.50 euros.'

'Here you go, the rest is for you.' 'Thanks! Have a nice day!' 'Will you wait a moment, please?' 'Yes, no problem.'

Silvia got out and went to Jochen's house. It was a big house with two floors, a garden and a garage. It was located in a very nice and quiet neighborhood. There were also stores where you could buy fruit, bread and everything you needed. Jochen's car was parked in front of the house. Was Jochen already at home after all? Had he perhaps called his brother?

Silvia was at a loss. If Jochen had gone home by car, why didn't she have a message on her cell phone? Silvia rang the doorbell three times, but no one answered.

She worriedly went to the house of her two friends Claudia and Veronika. But they were not at home either. And their cell phones were turned off. What was going on? Since they had met this monster, all their friends had disappeared.

Something had to happen. She couldn't call the police. She couldn't tell the police about a hairy creature in the forest. Besides, Jochen's car was parked in front of the door. But where was he? Was he injured or sick and in the hospital? She had to take the initiative and find him herself.

A few minutes later, she got back into the cab. This time she found a shorter route to the house by the lake. When she came out of the forest, she was paralyzed for a moment: there was light in the dark cottage. And Silvia knew exactly that she had turned off the light in the morning.

ZUSAMMENFASSUNG/ SUMMARY

Silvia and Jochen are searching the woods for the beast they are hunting for. Suddenly Jochen vanishes. Silvia is unaware of his whereabouts at this time. She leaves the park and heads back to the house. She is worn out and decides to take a nap in an old bed. The following morning, Jochen is still nowhere to be found. She has a lot of cause for concern. She uses her mobile phone to get in touch with Jochen on a regular basis. She travels to Jochen's residence via taxi.

However, Jochen is nowhere to be seen, despite the fact that his car is parked in front of the house. Even Silvia's close companions were nowhere to be found. Silvia is completely oblivious to everything that has taken place. In the end, she returns to the old house that is located by the lake.

FRAGEN

Wählen Sie nur eine Antwort pro Frage aus.

1) Silvia glaubt, das Wesen ist _____.

a. auf jeden Fall echt

b. wahrscheinlich nicht echt

c. Jochen

d. ein Yeti

2) Jochen verschwindet _____.

a. im See

b. auf dem Weg

c. in einem Dorf

d. im Wald

3) Silvia schläft _____.

a. im Wald

b. im Boot am See

c. in einem Bett im Haus

d. im Taxi

4) Als Silvia aufwacht, _____.

a. geht sie zum Dorf

b. rudert sie auf den See hinaus c. ruft sie Jochens Eltern an

d. ruft sie ihre Eltern an

5) Als Silvia zurück zum See geht, sieht sie _____.

a. das verbrannte Haus

b. Licht im Haus

c. das Wesen im Haus

d. Jochen im Haus

8) Silvia schläft _____.

WORTSCHATZ

hässlich	ugly
verfolgen	to pursue
Wir müssen uns trennen.	We have to split up
frei herumlaufen	to be on the loose
in die Nachrichten kommen	to be in the news
echt	real
verstecken	to hide
der Empfang	network coverage
einschlafen	to fall asleep
die Bank	bench
nervös	nervous
beschließen	to decide
Was für ein Glück!	How nice!

ANTWORTEN/ ANSWERS

1) Silvia glaubt, das Wesen ist _____.
b. wahrscheinlich nicht echt

2) Jochen verschwindet _____.
d. im Wald

3) Silvia schläft _____.
c. in einem Bett im Haus

4) Als Silvia aufwacht, _____.
a. geht sie zum Dorf

5) Als Silvia zurück zum See geht, sieht sie _____ .

b. Licht im Haus

ENGLISCH

1) Silvia thinks the creature is _____ .

b. probably not real

2) Jochen disappears _____ .

d. in the forest

3) Silvia sleeps _____ .

c. in a bed in the house

4) When Silvia wakes up _____ .

a. she goes to the village

5) When Silvia goes back to the lake, she sees _____ .

b. Light in the house

SCHLUSSFOLGERUNG/ CONCLUSION

Ach endlich! Wie war es?

Now that we've covered everything there is to know about the German stories and how to enhance your *LESEN* (reading skills) by reading them in basic in a variety of contexts, we sincerely hope that you had a good time reading these stories from our book, **'Short Stories for Adult Beginners: Become Conversational Today with Fun and Exciting Stories!'**, because we sure did!

Our journey has been like riding a rollercoaster with all of the German *Grammatik*, reading, and writing, as well as a lot of other German-related information.

'Übung macht den Meister,' as the saying goes, and at this point we can say with absolute certainty that you are the master of German. But, keep in mind that it is always essential that you keep learning German and maintain your flow.

Es was spaßig! Our journey of learning German has now come to a close, and it was everything we hoped for—fun, *interessant*, interactive, and insightful.

Sind Sie aufgeregt? Because we are and keep practicing the German language, *jetzt* until we see each other again!

Tschüss!!
Bis bald!

🎁 Access Your Exclusive Free Bonuses!

Congratulations on the purchase of your new book by Explore To Win!

As a thank you, we are thrilled to offer you incredible bonuses of significant value.

To access these valuable resources, simply scan the QR codes below.

BONUS #1
German Flashcards + Audiobook & More

BONUS #2
German Email Crash Course: Speak 10 Sentences in 3 Days

Remember, these bonuses are exclusively available to customers like you, complementing your language-learning experience perfectly.

Thank you for choosing Explore To Win, and we wish you great success as you embark on your linguistic adventure!

Made in the USA
Middletown, DE
30 August 2024

60041100R00126